The Jazz Exiles

The Jazz

Bill Moody Foreword by Stanley Dance

Exiles

American Musicians Abroad

University of Nevada Press ▲▲ Reno / Las Vegas / London

University of Nevada Press,

Reno, Nevada 89557 USA

Copyright © 1993 Bill Moody

All rights reserved

Book design by Richard Hendel

Printed in the United States

of America

The paper used in this book meets the requirements
of American National Standard for Information
Sciences—Permanence of Paper for Printed Library
Materials, ANSI Z39.48-1984. Binding materials were
selected for strength and durability.

Library of Congress Cataloging-in-Publication Data

Moody, Bill, 1941–

   The jazz exiles : American musicians abroad / Bill
Moody ; foreword by Stanley Dance.

     p. cm.

Includes bibliographical references and index.

ISBN 0-87417-214-4 (cloth : alk. paper)

1. Expatriate musicians—Europe.   2. Expatriate
musicians—Japan.   3. Jazz musicians—United States.
4. Jazz—History and criticism.   I. Title.

ML385.M63 1993

781.65′089′13—dc20   92-26936

              CIP

              MN

9 8 7 6 5 4 3 2 1

This one is for Jo

The music, it's something

you can give only to those

who love it . . . it's for

giving. But there has to be

somebody ready to take it.

— Sidney Bechet

Contents

Illustrations

Foreword

From the beginning jazz musicians seem to have been as bold and adventurous as their music. They were soon heard not only throughout the United States, but also in Europe, Russia, Egypt, and China. Finding a friendly welcome and living conditions to their liking, some of them inevitably took up residence abroad.

The pioneers of the twenties were followed in the thirties by frequent visits and tours of bands and artists with established reputations, such as Louis Armstrong, Duke Ellington, Fats Waller, Coleman Hawkins, Benny Carter, and Jimmie Lunceford. After World War II, air travel changed the whole picture. No longer was it necessary to spend nearly two weeks in crossing and recrossing the Atlantic. As a notable result, musicians living in Europe never felt cut off and far from home. In addition, many had concluded that European audiences were more appreciative than the ones found back home.

Having lived in Europe for more than half my life, I explain the latter belief by the fact that long after Americans had begun to take jazz for granted, it remained something of a novelty to Europeans. The Duke Ellington Band, for example, was a sensation in England in 1933, but did not return there for a quarter of a century. Quite apart from the nearly six years of war that intervened, there was never the abundance of jazz to be heard on the air or in person that there had been in the United States. As a consequence, its greatest admirers, served mainly by 78 RPM records, were probably more intense—or, in the minds of their detractors, even fanatical—in their appreciation of the music.

After World War II, however, other conditions changed. The advent of bebop caused a second major division in both the music and the audience. There were more musicians playing jazz of one kind or another, but as educational facilities multiplied, work opportunities steadily diminished. Only a handful of regularly constituted big bands received enormous publicity and gave an illusion of health, but for most musicians, these bands offered merely a single night's work.

The jazz musician naturally goes where the business is, or more bluntly, where the money is. There were opportunities in Europe, especially for black musicians, who generally found less racial discrimination there. (Oddly enough, this had been the case even in the thirties, when London and Paris were the hubs of large colonial empires.) As Bill Moody makes clear, the self-exiled Americans enjoy star status at first, but eventually tend to become "locals." Yet the majority are like Johnny Griffin, who is quoted as feeling he "could have a more dignified life in Europe."

A big question is raised and largely answered in *The Jazz Exiles*: Why have such great artists as Sidney Bechet, Don Byas, Ben Webster, and Kenny Clarke preferred to live and die there?

Stanley Dance

Preface

This book deals with the phenomenon of American jazz musicians touring, working, and most important, living in Europe—and, as we shall see, Japan, Puerto Rico, and Morocco. This phenomenon has been referred to at one time or another as an exodus, the most important jazz movement in the post–World War II era, and the third largest migration in jazz history. Regardless of the terminology or frame of reference, the fact remains that since 1919, and even before, American jazz musicians, some very famous ones, have spent a good portion of their careers and lives in Europe.

I have called this group of American musicians the "jazz exiles." Some people may quibble with the term *exile*, preferring perhaps, *expatriate*. Certainly journalists have used that term, but expatriate implies, in addition to withdrawing from one's country, a withdrawing of allegiance as well. This was rarely the case. Even Sidney Bechet, who spent most of his adult life in Europe, where he became a hero of the French, retained his American citizenship. "Every man has two countries," Bechet said, "his own and France." And, despite his often bitter feelings toward his homeland, Kenny Clarke remained an American.

Even current residents of Europe such as Art Farmer and Kenny Drew—neither have any plans to return home—remain staunchly American despite living in Vienna and Copenhagen, respectively. The rare exceptions I am aware of are singer Josephine Baker and trumpeter Arthur Briggs, both of whom became French citizens.

The exile experience is, however, not confined to jazz musicians. Malcolm Cowley writes extensively of the American writers in the twenties in the *Exile's Return*. Exiled writers have themselves written about the experience and are careful to distinguish the difference between the terms expatriate and exile.

"The expatriate," wrote author Mary McCarthy, herself an exiled writer, is "a rather hedonistic escaper. The exile on the other hand is like a bird forced by chill weather at home to migrate but always poised to fly back." Exile, then, seems more appropriate given the music's treatment in America.

"Distance lends perspective though not enchantment to the exile," wrote Andrew Gurr, when discussing exiled writers. Nevertheless, many of the musicians concede Gurr's position:

> The most obvious benefit is of course the insight which distance gives. The exile gains not only the perspective which allows him to see his home clearly but he also has immediate and pressing comparisons to make. . . . The exile does not leave home with the intention of acquiring the superiority of the international traveler. . . . The exile leaves on an impulse to escape, not enjoy travel.[1]

As Art Farmer says when asked about life on the road, "I don't know anybody who enjoys traveling when they've done it for forty years."

Whether self-imposed or not, living in exile was one strategy employed by many American jazz musicians when faced with the dilemma of staying home to run a tailor shop, eking out a living at an innocuous day job, or going to Europe and playing jazz.

Curiously, despite being acutely conscious of the experience and what it has meant to his or her career, I have never heard any musician refer to himself as either an expatriate or an exile. These musicians discuss the exile experience freely but generally as, "the time I spent in Europe," or, "my life in Europe." There are some, however, who say that as with other artists, jazz musicians live in a kind of exile in their own country. Self-exile is perhaps, then, not a choice but rather a condition of the powerless. Given the numbers and the renown of the musicians, it is a strategy that calls for closer examination.

In addition to research and interviews, I have included in this study a considerable portion of my own experience in Europe. As Cowley wrote, "I felt justified in recounting my own adventures because they were in some ways representative of what was happening to others." I think it's worth noting from the outset that, although I was literally plucked from a classroom at the Berklee College of Music to tour with pianist Jr. Mance and singers Jimmy Rushing and Johnny Hartman, I was by no means a well-known musician to European audiences or musicians when I arrived in 1967. Yet for three years, I recorded and performed jazz almost exclusively with other American musicians as well as Europeans.

I returned from that first sojourn in 1970 and reflected on an experience that raised several questions in my own mind. How many jazz exiles were there? When had it all begun? And most important, why were many of the major names in jazz spending large chunks of their lives in foreign countries performing a music that is uniquely American in origin?

For the answers my research took me back to Europe and led me on a trail that stretched from the legendary Sidney Bechet to Donald Bailey, one of the more recent additions to the list of jazz exiles. From New Orleans to Nice, the picture that emerges suggests that until recently—and the jury is still out—America's only original art form has been regarded as such everywhere but in America. Jazz was born an unwanted child, scorned by its mother country, forced to go abroad to earn a living. Consequently, many of the leading exponents of jazz were, and still are, more welcome, more appreciated, in foreign countries than in their native land.

In the pages that follow, it is my intention to chart the movement of American musicians to Europe in a historical perspective and examine the exile experience from a number of viewpoints: musical, racial, sociological, psychological, and economic, all factors that are part of this chapter in jazz history. This is not intended to be a history of jazz. The response to exile is as varied as the musicians themselves. The musicians on whom I have focused have played—and still play— a significant role in the development and shaping of jazz.

Whether or not America's rejection and neglect of its own music produced the jazz exiles remains a point of contention.

James Lincoln Collier, the most outspoken opponent of this position, writes in *The Making of Jazz*:

> It has long been taken for granted by jazz writers and musicians
> that there has always been greater sympathy and understanding
> for jazz abroad than in its homeland. The assumption is simply un-
> true. . . . Briefly put, Europeans began to understand what jazz was

all about in the late 1920s and early 1930s. Although by 1930 there were a handful of ardent and knowledgeable jazz fans in England and more on the Continent a few years later, the actual audience for the music was tiny.[2]

Yet in the same book Collier quotes Duke Ellington returning from a European tour in 1939.

Ellington came home filled with good spirits. "Europe is a very different world from this one," he said. "You can go anywhere and talk to anybody and do anything you like. It's hard to believe. When you've eaten hot dogs all your life and you're suddenly offered caviar it's hard to believe it's true."[3]

When discussing Ellington's earlier tour in 1933, Collier writes: "No London hotel would take eighteen blacks. This was the first in a series of dents that the reputation, among the musicians, of European racial fairness would receive."[4]

In the next sentence, however, Collier tells us Ellington was allowed into the prestigious Dorchester, and the other musicians were scattered around a number of small hotels and rooming houses.

The point here, it seems to me, is that for whatever reason or condition, it *was* better in Europe; hence, the migration of scores of black American musicians to Europe.

In another work, *The Reception of Jazz in America*, Collier calls the European acceptance of jazz and its musicians a myth, perpetrated primarily by the political left. There are, however, a number of contradictions in Collier's argument. For example, he admits, "Jazz suffered a second slump in the mid to late 1960s and early 1970s in the face of the tremendous rock boom."[5] The rock boom Collier refers to was only one of the factors that caused a wave of musicians to head for Europe. The Vietnam War, political unrest, and a growing climate of racism were certainly other reasons for many of the exiles' departure.

Collier also clearly states, "The musicians, then, were the first to believe that things were better in Europe." Whatever the case, there is no other plausible explanation for a Sidney Bechet, Don

Byas, Kenny Clarke, Dexter Gordon, Art Farmer, Red Mitchell, or Phil Woods choosing to live in Europe. Although some critics and historians dispute the position that jazz was better received in Europe than America, and consequently provided a more favorable environment for the music, and a less hostile one for its black musicians, there is ample evidence from these musicians to suggest that support for this claim is valid. Whenever possible, I've let them speak for themselves.[6]

Acknowledgments

I would like to thank the following musicians for their time and patience in allowing me to conduct extensive in-person and telephone interviews: Donald Bailey, Garvin Bushell, Jay Cameron, the late Eddie "Lockjaw" Davis, Nathan Davis, Bob Dorough, Art Farmer, Bud Freeman, Jon Hendricks, Keith "Red" Mitchell, Mark Murphy, Phil Woods, and Louise Bushell.

Also thanks are in order to Lewis Porter at Rutgers University for his encouragement and for opening the doors to the Institute of Jazz Studies; to Dan Morgenstern and Ed Berger for their help at the institute; and to Billy Taylor and Stanley Dance for their encouragement.

Finally, I want to express special appreciation to those members of the University of Nevada, Las Vegas, Department of English who supported this project in a number of ways: to department chair Chris Hudgins; John Irsfeld, thesis director; Wilber Stevens, James Hazen, and the late Arlen Collier during the project's infancy as a master's thesis.

Prelude

In the fall of 1967, I made the first of several journeys to Europe. I had been invited to participate in the Prague International Jazz Festival and planned on a month-long stay with a Czechoslovak jazz ensemble under the direction of Gustav Brom. The month of touring and recording stretched into a three-year stay in Europe, primarily because of that first experience in Prague. I was, of course, neither the first American musician in Czechoslovakia nor the first to guest with Brom, having been preceded by clarinetist Edmund Hall and trumpeter Ted Curson.

At the 1967 Prague Festival, the Brom orchestra shared the program with a big band from the Soviet Union and a variety of small combos from other Eastern Bloc countries. Also on the bill were the Charles Lloyd quartet; American singer Mark Murphy, backed by a British trio; and a band co-led by Belgian pianist Francy Boland and the late American drummer Kenny Clarke.

I knew Clarke had been living in Europe since 1956, but I was astonished at the number of American musicians in the band. Besides Clarke, Benny Bailey, Johnny Griffin, Jimmy Woode, Sahib Shihab, and Nat Peck—forgotten names from the backs of old album covers— were now doing very well in Paris, Munich, Stockholm, Copenhagen, Zurich, and London.

The band included, in addition to Americans, the best of British and European musicians: Ronnie Scott, Derek Humble, Jimmy Deucar, and trombonist Ake Persson, who was often used by Duke Ellington on European tours. In its eleven-year life, the Clarke-Boland aggregation recorded thirty-six albums. One featured Stan Getz; another, Carmen McRae. But only two were distributed in the United States, so most Americans know little of the band's existence.

Singer Mark Murphy was also at this time living permanently in London. His pianist, Gordon Beck, would eventually join Phil Woods's European Rhythm Machine, formed during Woods's five-year stay in Europe.

The scheduled month with Brom's orchestra became a year during which I found wildly enthusiastic and knowledgeable jazz fans throughout Czechoslovakia. I experienced what was for me an entirely new and alien concept—working with a radio band that was *required* to record several jazz pieces each month.

Brom's orchestra, based in Brno, about one hundred miles north of Prague, included several fine arranger-composers and a repertoire of arrangements from Count Basie, Duke Ellington, Woody Herman, and Brom's special favorite, Stan Kenton. These were charts meticulously copied from records. There were many such bands in Europe, as I was to eventually learn, employing American musicians and arrangers. The year with Brom was an eye-opening experience in several ways.

First, the caliber of musicianship in Brom's band was very high indeed. There were some first-rate jazz soloists in the band, several with intensive conservatory training. The bassist at the time, and the person most responsible for my being in Czechoslovakia, was recently returned from a year's scholarship to the Berklee College of Music in Boston.

Milan Rezabek, after he defected in 1968, became one of several Czechoslovak bassists to make their mark on jazz. Rezabek worked with Earl Hines and Teddy Wilson. Miroslav Vitous and George Mraz were two others, added to a list that includes Stephane Grapelli, Django Reinhardt, and Joe Zawinul, who dispelled the myth that jazz can only be played authentically by Americans.

Second, I was continually impressed by the audience for Brom's band. By this time Gustav Brom had led a band for over twenty years and his followers were legion. We traveled throughout Czechoslovakia and played at everything from dances to jazz concerts. As the only American member of the band, I became something of a novelty and was continually singled out to verify, if I could, some fact or other about a jazz recording session, a musician, or a composition. There were a number of times when I wished for a copy of Leonard Feather's *Encyclopedia of Jazz*.

That year also included a tour of the Soviet Union (it was an annual event for Brom), a two-month odyssey that covered every major city and packed concert halls for all the performances. Again, I was by no means the first American musician in the Soviet Union. Benny Goodman had toured in 1962; Earl Hines in 1966; Sam Wooding and Sidney Bechet in 1926.

As Frederick Starr points out, "Between 1919 and 1924, black and white jazz bands penetrated every major city in Western Europe, and then beyond to such far flung centers as Istanbul and Shanghai."[1] Tashkent was the closest we came to Shanghai, where hordes of jazz fans, many looking like Ghengis Kahn, turned out for the outdoor concerts, and as Phil Woods says, "were probably intrigued by the rhythms."

Again, the audiences in the Soviet Union were knowledgeable and appreciative; the musicians were eager for talk and play, although they were inhibited by possible reprisals that precluded much contact off the bandstand. We did, however, participate in several impromptu jam sessions, especially in Moscow where jazz was firmly taking hold with a number of Coltrane disciples. This tour was, however, an event not nearly as surprising as Brom's announcement that his guest for the 1968 Prague festival was to be trumpeter Maynard Ferguson, who at the time was living in Bradford, England.

There was, unfortunately, a historic event that preceded the jazz festival. Despite Ferguson's appearance, the Soviet invasion of Czechoslovakia in August 1968 dampened the jazz scene considerably. Jazz and politics don't often mix, but I suddenly found myself embroiled in this country's plight. I had gone to London for a short vacation during the time Soviet tanks rolled into Prague. I heard the news of the invasion on the Voice of America broadcast. It was some time before I could get through to Brom, who sadly told me of the tragic events. In Brno, the Soviet troops had stormed the radio station and confiscated some of the instruments. A number of the musicians left immediately for nearby Vienna but returned when calm was restored. I had left my drums and personal effects in Brno since I planned to return, but it wasn't until the 1968 festival, delayed until December, that I was able to do so.

Ferguson's reception was overwhelming, and even though the trumpeter managed to get himself locked in a bank, we recorded two albums with Brom and, later, a special for Czechoslovak television.

Ferguson went back to England; I moved on to join a sextet led by Austrian saxophonist Hans Koller in Hamburg, Germany. Koller had been a guest with Brom several times during the year I was there, so when the vacancy came up, he offered the job to me.

In Hamburg, I found more exiles: two fellow Californians, altoist Herb Geller and drummer Jimmy Pratt. Both were on staff contracts with Nord Deutsche Rundfunk, Radio Hamburg. In addition to working with Koller's group at the German State Theater, which included American altoist Frank St. Peter, I often played at a small jazz club as part of the house rhythm section, backing visiting Americans. The Jazzhaus was one of a number of small jazz clubs scattered about Europe that featured American musicians.

During my tenure at the club, Leo Wright, from one of Dizzy Gillespie's small groups, and on vacation from Radio Berlin, appeared twice. Wright had been living in Berlin since 1964. "Sure I'll go back if the opportunity presents itself, the financial opportunity that is," Wright said. "That's where it is. I get two months off and vacation pay in Berlin, and I can tour."

Trumpeter Carmel Jones, an alumnus of Horace Silver and Gerald Wilson, was also living in Berlin. Hank Mobley, a former Miles Davis sideman, flew in from Paris, and trumpeter Charles Toliver passed through on leave from Max Roach's band. Saxophonist Johnny Griffin brought drummer Philly Joe Jones for his visit and trombonist Slide Hampton was also a frequent visitor to the club.

This interlude in Hamburg was broken only by a return visit to Czechoslovakia for a tour of Germany, Switzerland, and Austria with Brom's band. This time, however, we backed Ray Coniff, who brought along only his arrangements and two musicians: trumpeter John Best and alto saxophonist Skeets Herfurt. Brom augmented his band with additional musicians and added sixteen singers from Prague for Coniff's vocal arrangements. A live double album was recorded, but the highlight at the concerts was the small group dixieland outings with the Best-Herfurt frontline and the normally commercial Coniff on trombone.

As my second year in Europe drew to a close, I received word from Maynard Ferguson that singer Jon Hendricks was not only living in

Ben Webster (Ken Whitten Collection)

England but in search of a drummer. By the time I arrived in London, the former leader of Lambert, Hendricks & Ross was working six nights a week in a basement club in Soho. When we later toured Sweden, we were joined by bassist Red Mitchell, who was then beginning the first of more than twenty-four years residence in Stockholm.

Everywhere I looked, there were American jazz musicians living and working in Europe. Most were, like myself, in no hurry to go home, and with good reason. These American musicians in Europe were accorded respect, sometimes star treatment from European jazz fans, and enjoyed ample opportunities to perform what Max Roach has called "America's classical music." I realized, though, that many of the musicians I met and worked with during this period were forgotten names back home, however much in demand they were in Europe.

Saxophonist Stan Getz, who found himself an exile in Denmark for three years (1958–61), offers an explanation seconded by many musicians. "It [jazz] has suffered an unusual fate—misunderstood in the land of its birth, too often its buoyancy and rhythmic thrust have been confused with pushiness and arrogance. People involve themselves with its superficialities without digging for its soul. No wonder many of our best and brightest, in order to survive, had to seek haven in Europe."

Getz also poses an often unanswered question. "Why did a marvelous saxophonist like Ben Webster have to waste his last years in Europe when his value as a teacher could have been put to such great use in some of our schools?"[2] Why indeed?

Phil Woods ponders the same question and offers a possible solution. "Why don't we have a jazzman-in-residence in universities? Why did Ben Webster die in Europe alone? Why wasn't he given a post? Jazzman-in-residence—give him all the beer he wants and a room. 'Ben, you don't have to do nothing. Just stop by the jazz department if you feel like rapping with the kids.' Now you know human nature and so do I. You'd make the man so proud he'd probably cool his drinking. He'd live longer. He'd contribute to the kids. We don't think of these things. They're afraid to take a chance. Maybe Ben would go ape. Well, we've had poets go ape on campus before; that's very chic for a poet to go ape on campus."[3]

Woods, of course, is not talking about the many jazz musicians who have since gone the academic route and do have residencies on university campuses. Nathan Davis, David Baker, Max Roach, Jackie McLean, Don Menza, and Billy Taylor are current examples.

The question of why American musicians remain in Europe was answered well by trombonist Jiggs Whigam of Stan Kenton's band, who spent several years with a radio orchestra in Cologne. I'd only been in Europe a few days when he told me, "The longer you stay, the harder it is to go home."

One

The Road to Europe

The Road to Europe

Sam Wooding's band (Courtesy of Louise Bushell)

■n 1919, when Will Marion Cook arrived in England for the start of an extensive European tour, the newest member of Cook's Southern Syncopated Orchestra was a then unknown young clarinetist named Sidney Bechet. According to a number of sources, Bechet, who had been reluctant even to make the trip, was kidnapped by Cook.[1]

When Cook returned to America several months later, Bechet stayed on, that time for three years, and became not only the first great soloist in jazz, but the pioneer jazz exile.

Bechet bought his first soprano saxophone in London, and eventually he settled permanently in France. He became a national figure on par with such French celebrities as Edith Piaf and Maurice Chevalier. His records sold over a million copies in France alone, a street was named in his honor, and his wedding, in 1951, was the social event of the season and rivaled that of actress Rita Hayworth and Aly Kahn the previous year. All this, despite the fact that Bechet was an American. His place in music history is now assured, but it was Bechet's period of prolonged exile in Europe that began an entire chapter of jazz history.

The term *exile* conjures up images of dethroned kings or deposed Third World leaders, not jazz musicians. Exile, however, is as much a part of the jazz experience and history as improvisation or one-nighters. Following Sidney Bechet's example, American jazz musicians have been making the Atlantic crossing in a continuing exodus that is now regarded as the third largest migration in the history of jazz.[2]

Born in New Orleans, jazz developed and matured in Kansas City, Chicago, and New York. But ironically it was Europe that nurtured the music and provided its artists wider audiences, more aware and knowledgeable fans, and perhaps most important, the opportunity for artistic exploration.

The picture that emerges is painfully clear. The music that was created solely in America was, and still is to a great degree, neglected in its native land. Rejected, or at best neglected, in his own country, the American jazz musician departed for the capitals of Europe. In Paris, Stockholm, Copenhagen, London, and Amsterdam, American jazz musicians found appreciation, acceptance, and acclaim. Black musicians found in addition a far less hostile racial atmosphere.

"America," says singer-lyricist Jon Hendricks "is the only country in the world that denies its cultural heritage—jazz."[3] Hendricks's words are an echo of yet another jazz pioneer, trumpeter Dizzy Gillespie. In a provocative essay for *Esquire's World of Jazz*, Gillespie wrote:

> Jazz is too good for America. The people who gave birth to this wonderful music have never fully acknowledged it as an important part of our culture. As an American, I'm deeply sorry that foreign countries have beaten us to the punch in exploiting so fully a music we originally created.[4]

If the feelings of Hendricks and Gillespie seem a harsh overstatement of the case, for scores of musicians their sentiments have the familiar ring of truth and are supported by the experiences of Sidney Bechet, Don Byas, Coleman Hawkins, Ben Webster, Bud Powell, Kenny Clarke, Stan Getz, Chet Baker, Dexter Gordon, Phil Woods, Thad Jones, and a host of other American musicians who, for varying periods of time, became jazz exiles. These musicians found in Europe not only a warm welcome, but a zeal for jazz rarely encountered in America. If they returned—and many did—they discovered America had taken its cue from Europe. A case in point is tenor saxophonist Dexter Gordon.

On an October evening in 1976, Gordon, one of the acknowledged masters of the instrument, opened to overflow crowds at the Village Vanguard in New York City. The eager fans who lined up outside in the brisk night air were there to witness Gordon's return, while the press coverage was led by the *New York Times* and the *Village Voice*. A recording session was already in the works and a tour of major American cities was in the planning stages.

Dexter Gordon was back from a journey that had begun in Los Angeles with the bands of Louis Armstrong, Lionel Hampton, and Billy Eckstine. Moving to New York, Gordon worked with Charlie Parker and led a wide range of small groups under his own name. Finally, Gordon landed in Europe. His return was not from a prison sentence or a prolonged illness—both had figured in his career—but from a period of exile in Paris and Copenhagen that had lasted for fourteen years.

After signing with Blue Note Records in 1962, Gordon left Los Angeles and relocated to New York. The move seemed to assure an already burgeoning career that had suffered its share of difficulties in the fifties. But a chance meeting with Ronnie Scott, the proprietor of what is now Europe's oldest established jazz club, changed Gordon's life.

"Ronnie offered me a month at his club in London," Gordon said, "and the possibility of some other dates on the Continent. I finally ended up at the Club Montmartre in Copenhagen and before I knew it, it was 1976."[5] Fourteen years. But Gordon's story is neither exceptional nor unusual.

"There's no place in the States I can do a television show with a sixty-piece orchestra, and then turn around and record with the same band," said singer Mark Murphy, whose unique talents place him high in the ranks of an elite corps of jazz vocalists. Murphy spent nearly a decade in Europe, and now makes his home in San Francisco.

"One of my later albums had only eight musicians. The arranger, Mitch Farber, made it sound like a big band, but when you work in as many night clubs with as many trios as I do, it's really a thrill to hear some strings behind you."[6]

Jazz is a regular feature of European television, but with the exception of rare programs on public television, one of the cable networks, or Billy Taylor's features on "CBS Sunday Morning," jazz has been virtually nonexistent for the American viewer. Defenders of American television argue that there is an equal shortage of ballet, opera, and classical music. None of these, however, are American art forms.

Murphy's explanation is more basic. "Money, greed, and paranoia that someone might change the channel for even a minute and you'd be the cause of it. You can get on the 'Tonight Show' if you're lucky, and they do have a fantastic band. But on all those shows, there's no reason not to have a jazz artist once a week—and maybe every third week, a jazz vocalist. But they don't. It's not their policy. But I don't kid myself, America is geared on money success. You just have to find a way to survive." For many musicians, the road to survival often leads to Europe.

"Jazz has moved to Europe," said saxophonist Bud Freeman, a fifty-year veteran of the jazz wars. "Actually, I didn't take all the work I was offered. Germany, Belgium, Holland, you name it, I've been there."

A charter member of Chicago's famed Austin High gang, that included Dave Tough, Jimmy McPartland, and Frank Teschemacher, Freeman spent six years in London before returning home to Chicago in 1980. While in Europe, Freeman toured extensively and recorded some twenty albums. But work opportunities aside, Freeman cites the serious acceptance of jazz in Europe and America's failure to follow suit as major factors in the decision of many musicians who opt for European exile.

"Oh, I think there's no question about it," said Freeman. "In many cases, especially in England, I've talked to symphony musicians who agree. I was very honored when the London Symphony gave a party for me, although I told them I thought they were way over my head musically. 'Nonsense,' they said. 'We could never do the things jazz musicians do. We can play the classical repertoire, and read anything at sight, but we can't do what *you* do.' Now I've heard that many times from many musicians I felt were superior to me. I don't think most Americans understand this. America is about fifty years behind Europe in its regard for jazz."[7]

Still another saxophonist, the late Eddie "Lockjaw" Davis, agrees with Freeman. A mainstay of the Count Basie Band for many years, Davis lived in Las Vegas before his death in 1986 but spent more than half of each year touring in Europe.

"Jazz is the only art form created in the United States," said Davis. "Everything else was brought over. The classics, opera, ballet, they were not created here. But jazz is considered an art form everywhere but America. Here, it's entertainment, so it's not recognized as art. We have organizations, jazz societies that are trying to give it a different image, but it's difficult. It's always an uphill battle for jazz."[8]

The number of jazz musicians today accorded the stature or financial security commensurate with the time, effort, and talent required to reach the level of musicianship essential to its performance is relatively small. With few exceptions, the jazz musician lives in a kind of limbo, somewhere between artistic status and financial security. Rock musicians make more money; classical musicians have more status.

Add to this the high attrition rate in jazz, brought about by the burdens of constant touring, indifferent club owners and promoters, and a modicum of artistic acceptance. The toll has been inordinately high, and resulted in the tragic loss of many outstanding musicians at the peak of their careers through ill health, drugs, or alcohol—the trinity of the road.

Charlie Parker, Billie Holiday, Bud Powell, Clifford Brown, John Coltrane, Wes Montgomery, Cannonball Adderly, and Bill Evans are but a few who offer mute testimony to the rigors of the road.

Louis Hayes, for many years the drummer with Cannonball Adderly, perhaps best describes life on the road and in the clubs.

> You like to give and your music is the thing that attracts people. I went through different stages with that. I used to feel very arrogant at one time, wouldn't talk. Then, other times, I was switched off in a different way. It is hard because sometimes you don't want to talk to anyone and there's nothing to do. Time on your hands, and with some people it can start funny habits. Like playing is something that's very hard to do, so if you drink, or smoke, or whatever at the same time, it doesn't work, at least not for me. You come off the stand feeling up—energy keyed up and have all this time. You're working but everyone else is having a good time enjoying you. It *can* be destructive when your art is taking place in these places.[9]

For the survivors, the options are limited. While George Benson, Chick Corea, and Herbie Hancock—all firmly rooted in jazz—made the crossover trip to the wider audiences and commercial success with the fusion of jazz and rock, numerous other jazz musicians flocked to the studios of New York and Hollywood. Sacrificing jazz for movie and television scores, or jingles hawking the Madison Avenue message, they often found that the worse the music, the better the pay.

The uncompromising jazz musician—Art Farmer, Johnny Griffin, Phil Woods are good examples—is left in the curious position of fending for himself. Vying for an audience, he carefully steps through the minefield of rock and all its stepchildren—soul, heavy metal, punk, new wave, rap—or country and western. For every financially successful Miles Davis or Dave Brubeck, or Herbie Hancock, or Wynton Marsalis, there are hundreds of musicians living at the bare subsistence level.

Like the American writers of the twenties who went to Europe and became known as Gertrude Stein's "lost generation," American jazz musicians took the road to Europe at a steadily increasing rate. Many of America's prominent musicians live and work almost exclusively in Europe. Some are well known before they arrive and are revered as celebrities. Others, faces in the sections of touring bands, like what they see and remain to become established stars in their own right, while remaining virtually unknown in their native land. As guitarist Jimmy Raney told Red Mitchell, "I've become a living legend—forgotten but not gone."

The program of any European festival reads like a jazz honor roll. American jazzmen are found in big cities, small towns, and even, occasionally, in Eastern Europe, where they are equally well known via black market recordings, jazz publications, and ironically, Voice of America broadcasts.

"What America needs is a Voice of America for Americans," observes saxophonist Phil Woods. "With the exception of our own people, we've educated the whole world about jazz."[10] Before his return to America in 1972, Woods spent five years in France. Since his return, he has won several Grammy awards and is a perennial winner of jazz polls.

The Americans in Europe represent a diversity of styles that range from the Chicago sound of Bud Freeman, to mainstream players like Phil Woods and Dexter Gordon, to the experiments in free jazz of Don Cherry and Burton Greene. Categories merge and dissolve as all share a common bond—the continuing search for artistic acceptance as jazz artists. The exodus began in 1919 with Sidney Bechet.

2

Early Explorers

Chick Webb's band (Courtesy of Louise Bushell)

The United States went to war in Germany in 1917. In that same year Nick LaRoca's Original Dixieland Jazz Band recorded and sold a million copies of "Livery Stable Blues," thus marking the arrival of jazz in Europe.

The ODJB later toured England in 1919 to sellout crowds. The band was unique simply because they were the first band to record, and consequently they received an avalanche of publicity. But as Chris Goddard points out, "their success proves that what passes for novelty is subconsciously what many people have been expecting for a long time."[1]

For jazz, the military bands of James Reese Europe's Hellfighters and Tim Brymm's Seventy Black Devils of the 350th Field Artillery played a far more important role in 1918. The bands of Brymm and Europe were immensely successful in France and given a good deal of publicity by the French press. The Hellfighters could even boast of Bill "Bojangles" Robinson as its drum major.[2]

Stories of big money and the absence of racial discrimination by returnees from these and other bands filtered back to New York and prompted other leaders to cross the Atlantic with their own bands. One such leader was Will Marion Cook, who played a vital role in Sidney Bechet's career. It was Cook who was responsible for Bechet's first visit to Europe.

Will Marion Cook grew up in Washington, D.C., in a largely middle-class environment; by any standards, he was an accomplished musician. As a child, he studied violin and eventually became a student of Anton Dvorak at the Berlin Conservatory. Later, he joined the Boston Symphony and was ultimately a candidate for the position of first violin with that prestigious orchestra. Hiring policies in the symphony at that time, however, precluded his promotion and proved to be a decisive factor in the formation of the Southern Syncopated Orchestra.

The Cook orchestra repertoire consisted of the classics, some of Cook's own compositions, and several ragtime numbers. Cook's goal seems to have been to show that black musicians were just as technically proficient as whites. Cook himself certainly had the training and credentials for such a venture. He was also one of the few classically trained musicians to possess a pronounced feeling for the blues. The one missing element in the Southern Syncopated Orchestra was a first-rate jazz soloist. Enter Sydney Bechet.

While performing in Chicago, Cook heard Bechet at a local club and enticed him to join his orchestra as the "hot" man. Cook's thinking was to feature Bechet much as W. C. Handy had used clarinetist Johnny Dunn. Bechet agreed but stayed only a few months before leaving to join Tim Brymm's Black Devils. During Bechet's absence, Cook set about reorganizing his orchestra in preparation for a European tour. He was set on having Bechet accompany him, but the stubborn Bechet was not interested and flatly refused Cook's offer. According to some sources, when reason failed, Cook had Bechet kidnapped and brought aboard the ship that was to take the orchestra to England.[3]

This scenario is disputed by other writers, although Garvin Bushell said, "Yeah, that sounds like something that could happen to Sidney." John Chilton, however, offers what is probably the real story: Cook simply threatened Bechet with litigation if he did not fulfill his contract.[4]

Bechet's impact in Europe was immediate and profound. The Southern Syncopated Orchestra arrived in England in July 1919 with the reluctant Bechet in tow. A young classical conductor, Ernest Ansermet, reviewed one of their concerts. In a glowing article for the *Revue Romande*, Ansermet declared Bechet "an extraordinary clarinet virtuoso."[5] In a more recent analysis of Bechet's playing, Gunther Schuller wrote, "Bechet's melodic lines had an inevitability that marks the master."[6]

While Bechet's initial visit to Europe may or may not have been with his consent, it was nonetheless a pivotal point in his life. He would remain there for much of the next thirteen years and become the first of the true jazz exiles.

The presence of Bechet in an orchestra the caliber of Cook's was something of a departure, considering that Bechet did not read music at all. The rest of the orchestra played entirely from written scores. Bechet's lack of formal training, however, did little to detract from his skill as a soloist.

The late trumpeter Arthur Briggs, who worked with Bechet in the Cook orchestra and later with Noble Sissle in Paris, offers some insight into Bechet's phenomenal talent. "In the Cook band, the truth is, the only improvising that was done was by Sidney. There was a curious thing about him. It was said that he couldn't read music, but I've seen him sit at the piano and play chords and call them off correctly. Now how did he learn to do that?"[7] The answer seems to be simply that Bechet was a genius, a natural musician, and that instance was not the first time he had amazed other musicians.

While in London, Bechet began to play the soprano saxophone on feature numbers with great success. Cook's band, however, was beginning to have problems. When Cook left for a tour of the Continent, Bechet stayed behind with another alumnus of the band, drummer Benny Peyton. Together, they organized a group called the Jazz Kings.

While Cook's orchestra eventually disbanded because of financial problems, Bechet flourished and was joined by several other members of the Cook orchestra who had also remained in England and found work with British bands. Still others, like drummer Louis Mitchell who formed a group also called the Jazz Kings, worked extensively on the Continent. Bechet played with all of them at one time or another but was finally forced to return to New York in 1921, when he was deported from England over an incident with a prostitute.[8]

Considering the circumstances and the severity of the penalty, racism seems to be the cause of this incident even though there is no hard evidence to prove it. In any case, Bechet returned to America. For the next few years, he toured with a number of bands, including Duke Ellington and James P. Johnson. For a short time he led his own group under the name of the New Orleans Creole Jazz Band.

In the fall of 1925, Bechet joined an orchestra backing a variety show, *Revue Negre*, led by Claude Hopkins and featuring singer-dancer Josephine Baker. The show opened in Paris, and although it was only moderately successful it proved to be a launching pad for Baker, who, like Bechet, remained in France and became an international star.

Bechet left the show to tour Russia, again with drummer Benny

Peyton. Here he ran into his old friend Garvin Bushell and trumpeter Tommy Ladnier, both then touring with Sam Wooding and *The Chocolate Kiddies*. Bushell recalls spending a good deal of time with Bechet and engaging in a friendly rivalry in breeding dogs.

Following the Russian tour, Bechet returned to Berlin, formed his own group, and toured Europe for the next two years before he eventually settled in Paris in 1928.

In 1929 he was again beset by personal problems and served eleven months in jail over a shooting incident at a Paris nightclub.[9] Upon his release from prison, Bechet spent another several months in Berlin before returning to New York.

Bechet worked again with Duke Ellington, a trio led by Willie "the Lion" Smith, and various other pickup bands. Hard times forced him to leave performing entirely at one point. He supported himself by teaching and operating a tailor shop in New York City with Tommy Ladnier. Here, as John Chilton reminds us, is the seed of all the jazz exiles:

> Here were two great black artists, one of them possessing talents that placed him amongst the finest natural musicians that America had produced, and they were forced by circumstances to become menials. Like true artists they had done their best to present the world with work that was untainted by commercialism, but they found no takers. They had played their music with supreme skill and it had lacked neither emotion nor expression, but their reward, for the time being, was to be ignored.[10]

Wary of Europe after two scrapes with the law, Bechet rejoined Noble Sissle in 1934 and spent the next several years and throughout World War II playing clubs in and around New York. Following the war, he made several working visits to Europe beginning in 1949, eighteen years after his troubles in Paris. There he was rediscovered, and made several trips back and forth across the Atlantic. He settled in France permanently in 1951, just in time for his third marriage.

Bechet's wedding to Elisabeth Ziegler was the social event of the year. Bechet had first met Ziegler in the early 1930s, and after a twenty-year separation, he was reunited with her on a tour of North Africa with Claude Luter. Ziegler moved to Paris, and she and Bechet began planning for the wedding, scheduled for August 1951. The ceremony was performed at the Cannes town hall, and among Sidney's witnesses was the American vice-consul. About four hundred guests then made a slow drive through the streets of Cannes in carriages before thousands of well-wishers and parading jazz bands. A twelve-foot model of a soprano saxophone was carried by two attendants. Afterward, the couple honeymooned in Juan-Les-Pins. The event was reported around the world.

With a street named in his honor and his records selling in the millions, Bechet was a national figure. "Who can blame him for settling in France?" said George Wein. "He was like a God there, bigger than he ever was in the States, yet he could have been as big as Louis Armstrong. But his suspiciousness alienated a lot of people; he had an inborn mistrust of managers and bookers." [11]

One of Bechet's pupils, writer Richard Hadlock, said, "Even after his triumphs in Europe in 1949, back in the States he was just another jazzman scuffling. Often when we went to the Automat after the job, Sidney would spot other musicians he knew and it would be like a party. Bull Moose Jackson was one I remember. But outside of musicians and 'inside fans,' Sidney was not a celebrity in his own country." [12]

The general public was hardly aware of any of this acclaim, though any Americans who traveled to France were soon enlightened. A visitor from the United States was quoted as saying: "Sidney could have become mayor of Paris if he wanted to. Crowds of people followed him through the streets. I was never so surprised in my whole life as when I discovered that a compatriot, whom I had barely heard of, had become the darling of the French. And I was quite embarrassed when asked questions by the French about Sidney and was unable to answer. They didn't understand why I, as an American, was so little informed about their idol." [13]

Active until the end, Bechet led an all-star band in Brussels in the summer of 1958, and died of cancer the following year. There was only one Sidney Bechet, but the adulation he received in Europe is typical of the high regard Europeans held for jazz and its artists. Bechet's experience paved the way for jazz exiles who would follow in his footsteps.

Other Cook Alumni

Like Sidney Bechet, trumpeter Arthur Briggs was to spend much of his life in France. After leaving Cook's orchestra, Briggs returned to the States for varying periods, but he too eventually settled in France. Briggs led his own bands before and after the war, and during the Nazi occupation he was interned in a concentration camp at St. Denis. Of the early days in Paris, Briggs says, "There was a nice little colony of blacks. We had artists, musicians, and boxers. We had certain bars where we met and we all got along nicely. We didn't come to Europe just for the life-style though. We had wonderful contracts as well." [14]

One of Briggs's visits to the States was with Noble Sissle's band, but he returned to Europe only months later. "The touring was tough with Noble. We'd sometimes play from nine in the morning. You see, America will kill you. New York is a bad place. That's why I stayed in Europe and that's why I'm alive today." [15] In 1964, Briggs was appointed professor at the cultural centers around Paris where he taught brass and saxophone. Briggs continued to teach and play until his death in 1991.

The experiences of Briggs and Bechet vividly point out that even at this early stage, Europe was not by any means a jazz utopia. Bechet's deportation and jail sentence in England and France, respectively, and Briggs's internment are two examples of some heavy dues-paying by American musicians for European residence.

Pianist-arranger Claude Hopkins, who went to Paris with the show starring Josephine Baker, also spent extended periods in Europe and cites, even then, the differences in European audiences. "The thing about Europe was the people were more receptive to the music than

Americans. They are today, and yet the musicians are better here in America. I guess it's because the beginning was here and it just developed." [16]

In addition to Hopkins, Briggs, and Bechet, many of the musicians who went to Europe with touring bands remained for long periods. Benny Peyton and Louis Mitchell, both with their own versions of the Jazz Kings, and drummer Buddy Gilmore were the most notable.

Multireed player Garvin Bushell was another who spent nearly three years in Europe with Sam Wooding. After long stints in Germany and France, the band toured Russia and South America before returning to America. Bushell toured Europe again in 1959 with Wilbur DeParis and then moved to Puerto Rico in 1967. In 1975 he relocated to Las Vegas, where he lived until his death in 1991.

While many of the bands of this period were show or dance bands, jazz was clearly an emerging force. The best players were being emulated by European musicians, particularly in France, where "throughout the 1920s there were black and white American musicians playing swinging music in Paris but it was not until the early 1930s that real evidence appeared of a well-rooted French jazz community of French musicians, fans (*les mordus*), and jazz writers." [17]

The presence of Wooding's and other bands paved the way for later American musicians and brought the assurance that jazz would always have a home in Europe.

On the vocal side, two other transplanted Americans, Josephine Baker and Alberta Hunter, achieved major stardom for their starring roles in shows throughout Europe. Both women spent many years in Europe, and during that period their careers were intertwined. For Baker, Europe became a permanent home.

Best remembered for long runs with the *Folies Bergere* and the *Casino de Paris*, Baker became a French citizen in 1937. During World War II, she was an ambulance driver and worked with the Free French underground. She was later awarded the Croix de Guerre and the Legion of Honor. Of the French people she said: "They have given me their hearts. Surely I can give them my life." [18]

Although not a bona fide jazz singer, it is doubtful Baker would have achieved anything like the stardom she found in Europe if she had remained in America. Although there are some inaccuracies, Baker's life was documented in an HBO film, *The Josephine Baker Story*, in 1991.

More closely linked with jazz is Alberta Hunter. After a professional debut at age fifteen, Hunter sang in a number of night spots around Chicago. During a five-year stint at Dreamland she worked with King Oliver and Louis Armstrong. She began composing and recording during that period, and one of her compositions, "Downhearted Blues," became a major hit and was later recorded by Bessie Smith. Hunter moved to New York and appeared in two shows on Broadway, *How Come* and *Change Your Luck*, in 1923.

Always in search of new plateaus, Hunter went to London with the aid of bandleader Noble Sissle. "When I went to Europe to work, I went because of Noble. It was impossible to just go over and work. You needed a work permit and that took six months. So Sissle told me that he'd arrange things, and he said, 'When you get to the border, mention the Lord Mayor's name.' So I did, and soon I was working in London."[19]

Engagements at the London Palladium and Pavillion followed, where Hunter came to the attention of Jerome Kern and Oscar Hammerstein. Hunter was offered the role of Queenie in *Showboat* with Paul Robeson at Drury Lane. *Showboat* was a major hit and Hunter was a worthy replacement for Josephine Baker in *Casino de Paris*. She later toured throughout Europe, and finally returned to England where she remained until 1939. After sixteen years in Europe, Hunter was back on Broadway, appearing with Ethel Waters in *Mambas Daughters*. The pairing was less than amicable, however, and Hunter left to join the USO, entertaining troops until the end of the Korean War.

In 1954, Hunter was again on Broadway as an understudy in *Mrs. Patterson*, but the death of her mother ended her performing career. At age sixty-two, she became a full-time nurse for the next twenty years until her retirement in 1977. But Hunter was not finished yet. At a party for pianist Bobby Short, Charlie Bourgeois, publicist for the

Alberta Hunter (Ken Whitten Collection)

Newport Jazz Festival, urged Hunter to contact Barney Josephson, the former proprietor of Cafe Society and the Cookery in Greenwich Village.

With Josephson's encouragement, the lady who introduced blues singing to Europe was launched on a new career as a jazz singer at age eighty-two. In the years following that opening, Hunter recorded the sound track for a motion picture, began work on her autobiography, and made many club and concert appearances.

In the fall of 1982, she returned to Europe for the Third Festival de Jazz in Paris. While there, she revisited the Hotel de Paris where she had lived in 1927. That tour included stops in Bremen, Germany, the Berlin Jazz Festival, and the Zurich Festival before circling back to Paris for the Grand Gala de Jazz. All at age eighty-seven.

The following year, she appeared at the 150 Club in Sao Paulo, Brazil, the site of several previous successes. In poor health now, Hunter's last engagement was in Denver, where she had to confess to the audience she couldn't finish the show. A British production company was planning to film her life story for a miniseries, and several albums were completed before her death on October 17, 1984. Always on the go, Hunter perhaps best summed up her life in jazz when she said, "I'm a female Marco Polo. I've traveled all over this earth."[20]

The Paris Scene

While Josephine Baker and Alberta Hunter were becoming stars in Europe, yet another singer, Ada Smith, better known as Bricktop, provided an outlet for scores of jazz musicians as hostess of *the* nightclub in Paris. Frequented by writers F. Scott Fitzgerald and Ernest Hemingway, and royalty such as Edward VIII, the Prince of Wales, Bricktop's was the focal point for Paris nightlife in the 1920s.

While Fitzgerald and Hemingway were fans only, the prince fancied himself a drummer and often sat in with the band, which included at the time Dave Tough on drums. The prince was enthusiastic but his efforts on the drums did not impress Tough, who remarked, "He

Dave Tough (Ken Whitten Collection)

might make a good king."[21] Tough had gone to Europe in 1927 and stayed three years to work with George Carhart. Later Tough worked in a trio with clarinetist Mezz Mezzrow, who would be living in France permanently by the early fifties.

Trumpeter Doc Cheatham was yet another of the early musicians

Doc Cheatham (Photo by Grant Collingwood, Ken Whitten Collection)

to spend a good deal of time in Europe with pianist Sam Wooding's band, backing *Chocolate Kiddies*. "I wanted to go," says Cheatham. "In those days it was a heck of a thing to get an opportunity to go to Europe with a band." Cheatham stayed three years but eventually it was musical considerations that prompted him to return to New York.

"I felt myself going stale. I wanted to progress and the only way was to come back home. You couldn't stay out of New York too long if you wanted to progress."[22]

But from a personal viewpoint, Europe had much to offer black musicians in particular, especially the absence of racial discrimination, the receptiveness of the audiences, and money. "There were lots of big jobs and money," says Cheatham. "More than in the States. There was no segregated musicians' union. When I was with Sam Wooding in Germany, we couldn't go out on the street because we'd always attract a crowd of fans following us."

Scores of musicians went to Europe during the late twenties and early thirties to discover for themselves the lure of the Continent. Shows like those that Josephine Baker and Alberta Hunter starred in were largely responsible for the spread of jazz in Europe, as many of the accompanying bands contained a number of topflight jazz players. Consequently, the music was introduced to many audiences who would normally not have heard it.

Some of the musicians, however, were disappointed by the lack of the pure jazz they were accustomed to hearing in Chicago or New York. These were the young white players of the day and included, besides Dave Tough and Mezz Mezzrow, Bunny Berigan, Muggsy Spanier, Jimmy Dorsey, and Bud Freeman. Freeman stayed only eleven days in Paris on a 1927 trip but eventually would spend a good deal of his professional life in France, and settle permanently in England in 1974.

Still others on the European scene during this period were Louis Armstrong and Benny Carter. After a tour of England in 1933, Armstrong had problems with his personal manager and remained in Paris until 1935.

Benny Carter spent three years in Europe, from 1935 to 1938, a stay which included a stint as staff arranger for the BBC, although he was not allowed to play in England.[23] He did, however, tour with Coleman Hawkins, who had arrived a year earlier and stayed until 1939. Trumpeter Bill Coleman was also in Europe for the first of many visits until he too settled permanently in France in 1948.

It was Carter, however, who made a major impact on the European jazz scene. Carter had no idea how long he would remain, but the

Coleman Hawkins (Ken Whitten Collection)

Bill Coleman (Ken Whitten Collection)

offer of a good salary from Willie Lewis, who had remained in Europe after leaving Sam Wooding, sounded fine. Carter was estranged from his wife, he had never been to Europe, and he had recently disbanded his own group. The more favorable racial situation in Europe was a factor in Carter's move.

"I suppose," he says, "that too played a part in my decision. Actually, I didn't suffer from so many racial incidents in America but I had my share and did have a sense of confinement. Or maybe I just became accustomed to such incidents and didn't let them get me down. I guess I may have felt that there was a plateau beyond which I couldn't go and that in Europe there were fewer limitations. But I won't say the racial situation ran me out of America."[24]

Carter arrived in Paris in 1935 and began playing immediately with Willie Lewis at the Chez Florence where he remained until March

1936, when he went to London. The Lewis band was not strictly a jazz band. In fact Carter recounts the music as "the sort Willie Lewis had been playing for some time—mainly melodies as written, with a little jazz occasionally." The club itself was an expensive supper club, an after-hours spot for wealthy Americans and Europeans, even royalty. "We used to play until the last customer left," Carter said.

Carter was already well known and admired by French jazz fans and musicians, thanks to author Robert Goffin's book in which he had rated Carter the "ace of alto saxophonists." Hugues Panassie had also written about Carter, and Charles Delaunay recalls Carter as a quick study of French. In addition to the Chez Florence gig, Carter was sitting with the quintette of the Hot Club of France that included guitarist Django Reinhardt and violinist Stephane Grappelli.

Despite the attention from British jazz fans, Carter could not go to London because of a mutual ban against British and American bands playing on each others' home grounds. Carter, however, was persuaded to come as an arranger as one way around the ban, but he could only stay three months at a time, an annoyance to both Carter and the jazz community.

"I had no experience arranging for strings," Carter recalls, "and the BBC orchestra made it mandatory." Carter had planned to enroll in the Royal Academy of Music to study composition, but he couldn't stay in the country long enough to complete the courses. Instead, he went to Rosamond Johnson, whom Carter had known in New York. Johnson was in London for several seasons to do vocal arrangements for Lew Leslie's annual Blackbirds productions, so in Carter's words, "I just went to him for the help I needed with strings."

Carter's agreement with the BBC, which took place within twenty-four hours of his arrival, called for recordings, publishing of his own works, and providing the dance orchestra with at least one arrangement for every week he resided in England. Carter provided some fifty such arrangments during his ten months from 1936 to 1938.

Carter's recollection of life in London is different but pleasant. He found an apartment near the BBC studios, although when he first arrived he was denied lodging at several hotels. Carter makes a valid point, however, when he says a musician visiting or living in Europe

Benny Carter (Ken Whitten Collection)

is in a special position. "I liked Europe professionally, musically, and socially. I've met many black musicians who speak of a special kind of freedom they feel there, escaping racial discrimination in America. While living in London and European cities, I always felt that if they'd had the same proportion of blacks as America they'd have had similar restrictions and problems." Today, Carter's remarks seem prophetic.

For the rest of his European stay, Carter worked in Holland, Denmark, and Sweden, where he told writer Neils Helstrom he missed America despite the racial discrimination, which Carter said was a well-known fact of life. "We are excluded from white restaurants and hotels but we do have very nice homes, and we are by no means lacking in culture, as so many people seem to think. We have our own culture."

Before returning to America, the British managed to obtain permission for one radio concert at the London Hippodrome, with little or no advance notice to the public. Carter was featured on his own "Waltzing the Blues." A second concert, on January 10, 1937, was heavily publicized and promoted and sponsored by the *Melody Maker*. All 1,600 seats were sold out in advance, and according to the jazz press, it was very much a Carter evening. He played and conducted most of the program, which featured his own compositions. A reviewer, besides lauding Carter's efforts, pointed out the impact his performance would make on good dance music and the prestige of British musicians.

Carter was, by this time, thinking about returning home. He wrote to a friend about missing New York and his boys. "I don't hear enough decent music to inspire me at all and I think what keeps me going now is the anticipation of my return to America. I really don't want to get too far behind, for when I come back I intend to have the greatest band ever."

In retrospect Carter realized the eventual limits in Europe, where American jazz was played and intensely appreciated but not so widely or as well as in America. It was just such an attitude that prompted many of the exiles to return when and if they were offered the chance.

"I wasn't sure I'd stay in America," Carter says. "I just thought I'd see how things were and I even left a few personal things in London." Carter had offers to stay, but unlike a number of other American musicians, he decided to go home. It would be 1954 before he returned to Europe with a Jazz at the Philharmonic tour.

The major players touring and living in Europe at this time—Hawkins, Ellington, Coleman, Carter—were all swing musicians. But the time was ripe for something new. What surfaced was a booming revival of traditional jazz. Sidney Bechet was rediscovered, and after years of swing, the return to the traditional sounds of King Oliver's Creole Jazz Band and the Louis Armstrong Hot Five recordings became the vogue. This continued throughout World War II, while

Europe was cut off from the developments already under way in New York. During the war years, American jazz was like a breath of fresh air and freedom, especially for the French in the face of the Nazi occupation. As the war continued, records were smuggled into Europe, but they were rare.

European audiences were totally unprepared for Dizzy Gillespie's invasion in 1948. Gillespie's tour was an event that sparked a new wave of modern jazz exiles.[25]

In America, bebop was revolutionizing jazz and setting the stage for Gillespie's tour with his first big bebop band. The impact of the band was tremendous and split Europe into two distinct camps: those who believed the only true jazz was traditional, and the champions of the bebop school. As bebop eventually won out, a steady stream of new jazz exiles would make their way across the Atlantic in the years to come.

3

*We had achieved
a name, money, and
we wanted to go
home and show off
– Garvin Bushell*

Garvin Bushell

J elly Roll Morton claimed to have invented jazz in 1902. That same year multireed instrumentalist Garvin Bushell might have been born on September 25, in Springfield, Ohio. Bushell was not quite sure. It may have been two years earlier. "I always thought it was 1902, but I found an old book of my mother's and it says: 'Garvin—1900.'"[1]

Whatever the date, Bushell could look back on a musical career that began with circus sideshows in 1916 and spanned seven decades, ending with the hotel house bands of Las Vegas. He made his home there from 1975 until his death in 1991. Bushell's career was a musical odyssey that included just about everybody from Bessie Smith and Fletcher Henderson to John Coltrane and Miles Davis.

For symphonic work, Bushell unpacked his bassoon and oboe for stints with Pablo Casals and the Puerto Rican Symphony, the New York City Ballet Theater, Radio City Music Hall, and the Chicago Civic Orchestra. When he wasn't playing or studying, Bushell was teaching, passing along his vast knowledge and experience to younger players like John Coltrane, after opening his own studio in New York in 1947.

"You know he [Coltrane] studied with me. He had mouthpiece troubles. He had already consulted Hawk [Coleman Hawkins] and he told him, 'Go and see Bushell.' He was never satisfied with that sound he produced, which was the thing about his playing besides runnin' up and down the horn and analyzing chords, which he could do. He was tremendous; he had a tremendous ear."

Bushell recorded not only with John Coltrane, but with Eric Dolphy and Miles Davis. On the *Africa Brass* sessions and *Trane's Modes*, the rumbling bassoon is Bushell. Although Bushell remembers those sessions vividly, there is a certain ambiguity in his attitude toward Coltrane.

"Coltrane had a hodgepodge of theory and some soul and creativity. But he could analyze chords, he knew chords well, he knew the outside of the chords, the neighboring tones. I thought he was great. He had fingers like lightning, but I didn't take too much to him. There was no story in John's playing, you had to be a musician to understand what he was doing. Takes a musician to appreciate that. A layman will say, 'I don't know what he's doing but he's doing it fast.'"

Of the Gil Evans–Miles Davis collaborations, Bushell remembered Coltrane and some of the other musicians not only for the music. "It was a trip because there were a lot of junkies in the band. Talented guys, arrangers, and some of the best players. Elvin Jones, Bobby Tricarico on bassoon with me, a great black French horn player. They had five horns. Those cats were in a trance until they sat down to play. It was weird."

And Miles Davis? "He had the worst chops in the world then. Is he still recording? I haven't heard any of those new things. Miles missed too many notes. I've been around too many trumpet players that what they intend to play came out. A lot of kids were missing notes because Miles did. He didn't know what the hell he was doing, but I admired him because he was a spunky little rascal. I'm a hot-rodder and Miles was too in those days. He'd put me on dates so we could either race to or back from the date."

Bushell saw a host of players come and go during his seventy years in music, but some musicians stood out in his mind. "I liked Cannonball [Adderly]. He had technique, quality, but I'll tell you the guy that I admire so much is one they always leave out. He played at Small's Paradise, he played altissimo, above everything. He can play on any kind of tune, and he wanted me to go into business with him. Earl Bostic, a great. Think Earl Bostic, Cannonball, and Benny Carter and you got it. I got some records of Phil Woods playing with Benny Carter. He could play the style that they play so well that they put him on those dates. He was the only white musician on those dates then. He was a copy, but so doggone good it was tremendous; he got it in the right places. I give Buddy DeFranco so much credit because nobody played clarinet like that. I give Stan [Getz] some credit because he did some things different from anybody else. Zoot was good, too, like Vido Musso, that Italian boy.

"I started with the circus and tent shows," Bushell said in his Las Vegas home. The walls of his studio are lined with photos, and there is a clutter of books and records and of course his ever-present horns, which he glanced at lovingly. They were his life since he began clarinet studies at age ten. "Those first gigs were with musicians who would become McKinney's Cotton Pickers. We were all kids but you know there were a lot of important things to jazz before 1920."

He looked at least twenty-five years younger than his age, and he moved and talked with the grace and wit of a man who has seen it all and is slightly amused by what he has seen. He still maintained a few students, but a stroke had slowed him considerably. Even these setbacks were not enough to keep him from the Las Vegas Jazz Month Summer Concerts in the park. "There's some good music here," he said.

Like most American jazz musicians, Bushell spent considerable time touring and living in foreign countries. He made his first trip abroad with pianist Sam Wooding and the show *Chocolate Kiddies* in 1925. "France woke America up to jazz," Bushell said, recalling a tour that resulted in a stay of nearly three years in Europe. "Europeans were acknowledging jazz even then. They were standing in line to see us. Paris, Prague, Berlin, Russia. We used to jam till dawn in Prague," Bushell recalled. "And after every show someone would invite us to dinner."

While in Berlin, Bushell would often spend his afternoons attending classical concerts. It was then that he decided to pursue symphony music as well as jazz. He studied with Henry Selmer in Paris and bassoon with Eli Carmen.

After a lengthy tour of South America, Bushell returned to New York in 1927 and embarked on an extensive free-lance career that made him the quintessential sideman. The music was good in the bands of Fletcher Henderson, Chick Webb, and Cab Calloway, but the money didn't always measure up. Racial discrimination was a way of life.

Returning from Europe with Wooding, Bushell says, "We had achieved a name, money, and we wanted to go home and show off. We didn't know we had it so good [in Europe]. We knew segregation existed but we were going to try and eradicate it when we got back to New York, you know, sow whatever seeds we could."

Bushell started his personal campaign by trying to integrate Loew's

Victoria theater. He sat downstairs in the restricted section and dared them to throw him out. "I wanted it," Bushell recalled. "They didn't know what I was. I had a cane, a homburg hat, and a British accent."

Bushell's first wife was a line dancer at the Cotton Club, another place Bushell could not go unless he was working. "Negroes were not allowed," he said. "The Apollo Theater was on 125th, so to go in you had to go around back to 126th, up the back stairs and sit in the gallery. Things were so bad in New York in the thirties and forties that when I worked the Roseland Ballroom with Fletcher Henderson, we had to go along the wall and down to the cellar on our breaks. We couldn't cross the floor like the white musicians, and we were the headline attraction at Roseland. New York was a very bad place in those days."

In 1937, Bushell joined drummer Chick Webb's band, but again the money was as short as the music was long. "We only got paid in theaters like the Paramount. It got better after Ella [Fitzgerald] joined, but we put Chick out of the car one night because he wouldn't pay us. It was four o'clock in the morning. We finally went back for him but he still wouldn't pay us, even after he got famous. Gene Krupa idolized him. He cried like a baby at Chick's funeral."

With Webb, Henderson, and Cab Calloway, the road trips and grueling one-nighters also meant enduring the South. For the most part those were experiences Bushell would rather forget, but they were as firmly etched in his memory as the race riot he witnessed as a child in Springfield.

"I'd come back a nervous wreck," Bushell recalled. "You don't look up from the music. At black dances they'd have white spectators. With Fletch, Chick, Cab, it was mostly white audiences. They liked you for what you could do. In East Texas, we traveled in Pullman cars. We were met by the promoter who told us they were going to take the sheriff and six deputies to protect us. One guy wanted to pay the sheriff. 'You can have this money to just let me get up there and hit that nigger [Cab Calloway] in the mouth.' We went to the cellars on the breaks and the valets stayed to protect the instruments. One time the editor of the *Longview Times* wanted to meet Cab. We went to see him the next day and had a good time—lunch, cigars, Scotch. But at the dance that night, we had to have guards to get us on the bus and take us back to our train. Those were vicious, ignorant people."

Years later, while visiting the South from Puerto Rico, Bushell found the attitude of many people unchanged. "In Biloxi, Mississippi, a cop told me I didn't have to stay in the black section. He took me to a motel, and said to the clerk, 'We got some niggers from Puerto Rico. Give them a room.'" Bushell sighed as he recalled the incident. "They know they're doing wrong, making you, a minority group, miserable, making a habit of doing that. There were some streets on the Army camp in 1941–42 when I was with the USO you couldn't walk on.

"We've survived all that. Many more blacks are tired of living in the ghetto; they're making changes, becoming professionals. Even language has changed, and thank God I've lived to see it all." Although perhaps not as openly hostile, things were no better back in New York, as Bushell discovered when he was called for a fifteen-week tour with Paul Whiteman's band. "They told me on the phone they wanted a bassoon and oboe, but when he [Whiteman] arrived and saw I was black, suddenly they needed a flute as well, which I didn't play. A white friend of mine got it. The union raised hell but I told them to forget it. This was 1948."

Bushell, however, continued his pursuit of symphony work and studied with the first bassoonist at NBC. Sometime later he was recommended for third chair with the New York City Ballet Theater. During the first three days of rehearsal, Bushell recalled that no one spoke to him. He responded with an old jazzman's trick and waited for a solo to show his stuff. "They spoke to me after that," Bushell laughed.

For Bushell and other black musicians, Europe, with the possible exception of England, was a different story when it came to prejudice. "We ran into a couple of spots, the attitude of some Germans. Swedes were more conscious of this color thing than anybody else but there was no such thing as segregation. France and Denmark were good; England was bad, you couldn't eat anywhere but Soho."

Despite the racial prejudice, the bad experiences, Bushell was, surprisingly, not at all bitter. "Let me tell you, with all the segregation we've had, we live better than any black people in the world. It's a

different story today. Blacks are whipping ass. Black mayors in southern cities and police departments." He was only tempted to remain
abroad once and that was in Morocco when the sultan urged Bushell
to stay by enticing him with his second love—fast cars. "The sultan
was a hot-rodder too. He must have had eighty cars in his garage.
All you could see was cars. 'You stay in Morocco, play jazz, I give you
Ferrari,' the sultan said." Unlike pianist Randy Weston, who lived for
many years in Morocco, Bushell passed.

"I thought about it, but after I'd been there I said with all the segregation and prejudice we have here, this is home and I feel better
because there are more of my people. Although they're black people
[Africans], we don't understand each other. We don't relate to each
other at all except for skin color. The background, the culture, the attitude, the philosophy is altogether different. I've been all over Africa
from top to bottom, including South Africa, forty-nine thousand miles
for the State Department. I remember when we were leaving Nairobi,
an East African waitress sarcastically asked, 'How does it feel going
back to your big, wonderful, strong country?' I said, 'Baby, it feels just
fine.'"[2]

On the other hand, Bushell is quick to point out the opportunities afforded him in Europe and Puerto Rico that were not readily
available in America.

"Let me tell you, I didn't have the opportunity to do the things I
did like when I was in Puerto Rico. I joined the symphony there. The
symphony things I did in the states—Radio City, the Ballet Theater—
were temporary. I was in Puerto Rico ten years under Pablo Casals
and Victor Tabor of Chile as conductors and also played jazz with
some of the best. I couldn't get that in New York, my own hometown."

What Bushell did miss while living abroad were the simple things—
language, the finesse of the shows, American culture. After a decade
in Puerto Rico it was time to come home. "My kids weren't speaking
English and wrestling with the language and culture was getting difficult, so I moved to Las Vegas, leased this house, and went back for
my family."

All Bushell knew about Las Vegas was what he'd heard from a pianist who had worked there in a lounge with the Treniers. "He told

me, 'You'll do great there with all those doubles and reeds you play.'
That's all I needed to hear." Bushell arrived on the Las Vegas scene
looking for work at an age when most people have long since retired.
He was seventy-four. What he found, however, was a variation on an
old theme.

"I worked at Caesars Palace whenever Sammy Davis, Jr., was in
town and they needed a black face in the saxophone section, but they
weren't hiring black musicians then for the house bands. I did some
work with Johnny Haig two or three nights in the relief band."

Bushell then concentrated once again on teaching. For five sum-
mers he taught at the Nevada School of the Arts under director Bill
Lowman, and his private practice grew to over sixty students. Playing decreased, of course, but Bushell seemed like Dorian Gray. "Music
has kept me young and every day is a new day for a bassoon player.
With Sam Wooding and Fess Williams I learned more about deport-
ment, and about thinking as a musician from Sam. My knowledge that
I gained from groups wasn't much. Individual study was best for me.
As far as jazz is concerned, I don't remember any ideas from Fletch.
Benny Goodman was one of my inspirations. I lean toward clarinet;
that was my favorite instrument and I listened to the records. But the
most fun was with Fess Williams. Fess was a good psychologist. He
knew how to handle kids and get you to work for nothing. I was the
straw boss but we were like brothers in that band. Plenty of fun."

Bushell felt jazz had changed, even the meaning of the word. "Using
that term, it's not jazz, it's gone a step further: the rock rhythm, the
kids buy that now. They buy the rhythm, not swing rhythm from that
old East Coast back beat. I don't say it's better. The guys today just
can't improvise as well, especially in this town [Las Vegas]. After Monk
[Montgomery] died, jazz [in Las Vegas] just quit."[3]

When asked about some of the younger players, such as Wynton
Marsalis, Bushell said, "He was born with that talent and he has unusual ability. I admire the young musicians; their technique is almost
flawless but they don't create too much. They're playing in the shadow
of Art Farmer but their range is greater, they take chances."

Bushell's autobiography, appropriately titled *Jazz from the Beginning*, was penned with writer Mark Tucker. In May 1991, the Las

Vegas Allied Arts Council presented a musical tribute to Bushell as part of its annual Jazz Month events. Throughout the evening, Bushell commented on the music and the musicians of each era portrayed. Not only was Bushell present for many of the developments in the music, but there are few musicians who have performed in so many different bands and styles.

—Las Vegas, 1988–91

4

Bud Freeman

Lawrence "Bud" Freeman's first trip to Europe was in 1927. His good friend Dave Tough was already in Paris, playing at Bricktop's, writing limericks with F. Scott Fitzgerald, and letting the Prince of Wales sit in. Freeman, however, was not impressed. He stayed only eleven days.[1] "There was more jazz being played in Chicago then, but now, I don't know. I've played all over Europe. There must be a hundred pubs in Britain alone that feature jazz."

A devoted Anglophile from early childhood, Freeman first went to England in 1962 with Dizzy Gillespie and Buck Clayton to play at the Manchester Jazz Festival. He was totally unprepared for the reception he was given by the English audiences as he walked on stage. He was already walking on air after being met at the airport by a cousin of the queen and driven past Eton College, Windsor Castle, and the green lawns of the English countryside. "I always knew I'd love England." He smiles in delight, remembering the experience.[2]

For nearly six years (1974–80), audiences throughout Britain and the Continent were treated to a firsthand look and listen to one of the greats of the so-called Chicago school of jazz. Freeman's popularity soared during this period with scores of club and concert appearances and an astonishing twenty albums to his credit.

Freeman was also a charter member of what has become known as the Austin High gang in Chicago. Other members were trumpeter Jimmy McPartland, clarinetist Frank Teschemacher, and the great drummer Dave Tough. Together, they formed the nucleus of the Chicago style.

"When I moved to London in 1974, it was like a dream. I had been with the World's Greatest Jazz Band since 1968. That name caused quite a stir," laughs Freeman, "but it wasn't really our idea. It was a great experience though because we were all soloists, so we had the freedom to do what we wanted. I was one of the original members of that band.

"Actually, I didn't take all the work I was offered," Freeman said. "I had a good agent and there are so many places to work. I'd like to do only six months a year, but something always comes up and it's difficult to refuse."

The career of Bud Freeman, or Uncle Bud, as he was known to scores of musicians, was a journey spanning six decades. From the mobster-owned clubs of the twenties' Chicago to jazz festivals in the south of France and the six-year residency in England, Bud Freeman was always on the move.

Freeman's first job was with Wingy Manone, but in 1927 a real break occurred. A recording session with another Chicagoan, guitarist Eddie Condon, proved to be the launching pad, not only for Freeman, but everyone on the date. A short time later, he joined the band of Ben Pollack and began a decade of shuttling between Chicago and New York.

Freeman's first move to New York was not without apprehension. He had received a telegram from bandleader Tommy Dorsey, but Freeman's current employer was a gruff Chicago club owner. Freeman wasn't quite sure how to approach him. He showed him the telegram from Dorsey and, to his great relief, the owner simply smiled and patted Freeman on the arm. "That's great, kid. You're on your way," Al Capone said. Freeman left Chicago (and Capone in search of a new saxophone player), and set out to make a name for himself in the world of jazz, a calling that endured for over sixty years.

In London, Freeman's home was a small residential hotel near Paddington Station and a short walk to Hyde Park. When not working, Freeman spent most afternoons at his favorite restaurant, a health food emporium near Carnaby Street that served vegetarian casseroles in a restful atmosphere, with classical music playing in the background. Just prior to his return to Chicago he talked about living in London and how he felt about returning to America.

"This is the best place to talk," he said. "The food is not only good, it's good for you." Though confessing to have tipped a few in his day, Freeman rarely drank then. He watched his diet, took long walks, and still played a respectable game of golf. He looked nowhere near his seventy-five years. Slightly built, he was an impeccable dresser and sported a narrow white mustache. But his most arresting feature was the mischievous blue eyes that sparkled when he talked about Europe. "I've been coming here since I was a kid," he said. "My mother was French, you see."

Freeman was a regular at the restaurant, and recognized by the serving girls who smiled shyly as he joked with them. Any conversation with Freeman is liberally sprinkled with stories of the jazz life— one of his favorite pastimes—but he could also discuss the merits of music and literature with equal ease. He spent a good deal of time reading, haunting the London bookshops, and taking advantage of the London theater whenever possible.

While Freeman worked with a number of big bands—Tommy Dorsey, Ray Noble, Benny Goodman, Pollack—he has always felt restricted by section work. For most of his career, he pursued the role of soloist with a rhythm section, but had no desire for his own permanent band.

"I'll tell you what it is," he said pensively, as always considering each answer carefully. "I wouldn't want to take over the custodianship of other people's lives. The more I respect a guy musically, the more I realize he can be difficult. It's only natural. I was a very difficult guy when I worked with the big bands because I wanted to be an individual. No, I just wouldn't want to do it. But now, there are so many great players around, all I really want is a rhythm section. Of course, you run into some bad groups now and then, but the only thing to do is be as polite as you can and hope for the best. I've experienced a funny thing though. If you're kind, by the end of the night, even bad players seem to play better."

As with many of the exiles, Freeman's success in Europe drew attention at home. A combination of events, most notably a summons from Chicago's mayor Jane Byrne, prompted Freeman to return to America in 1980.

"I have no idea how they found me," Freeman said, obviously pleased, "but I guess if people want you, they'll find a way. But a call from the mayor's office, inviting me to play at the Chicago Heritage Festival, well, that was quite a surprise.

There were other things as well. The Smithsonian Institution sent a reporter over to talk to Kenny Clarke and me. We taped for eleven hours, and that was really unexpected.[3] The *New Yorker* also did a piece on me, so finally, I wrote my brother in New York to find out what was going on. He told me I'd been away so long, I was getting famous at home. You don't always remember people are thinking about you but I guess it's true. These kind of things never happened to me in the States. The London press was very kind to me and I guess it eventually gets home, but there's got to be a strong reason to go back. There's got to be work."

Freeman turned serious when contemplating the idea of returning to America. He'd thought about it a great deal. "I'm sure Phil Woods and Dexter Gordon were tickled with the reception they got. I know I would be but I'm not entirely happy about the idea at the moment. I want to have a look around home and just see if there would be work. If there isn't, well, I'm going to give it about a year. I hope I'll be surprised, but I know I'm going to miss Europe.

"Europe has been my home, such as it is, for six years, although I've never owned a home of my own. Economics came into it as well. London has become extremely expensive these last couple of years. It costs me nearly fifty dollars a day for a hotel room, and it is certainly nothing luxurious. Americans don't get the tax break we once used to enjoy. So when I put it all together, I guess it's time. Of course, before I left, I was already booked in Europe for the following year—Germany, Holland, and Switzerland."

Freeman frowns as he remembers the travel involved in such a tour. Early morning planes, late night trains, often a new city each day. He's been doing it since he was eighteen, and he confesses it bores him no end. It's the playing he loves. "All the great players have a feeling and a love for the music. As I see it, jazz is all feeling."

Freeman communicated his feeling of the music in a variety of ways. "I really try to get to an audience," he said. "I find you have to tell them what you're going to do, sell it to them. That's why Louis Armstrong was such a success. He was always a master showman as well as a fantastic musician. Dizzy too. He knows how to get to an audience but that doesn't take away from his ability as a musician. For myself, I feel I'm playing better than ever, but I talk to an audience, tell stories, get them on my side."

Freeman, however, agreed with the majority of the exiles that jazz is not taken seriously enough in America. "I think there's no question about it. I run into Americans at festivals and clubs all over Europe who say to me, 'I wonder why we don't have anything like this at home?' My answer is always the same: I wonder too. America is about fifty years behind Europe in its regard for jazz."

After lunch, Freeman often walked across London, through Berkeley Square, past the exclusive shops, restaurants, and Rolls Royce showrooms of Mayfair, toward the expanse of Hyde Park, and to his hotel. "This is a lovely city," Freeman said, "but there are some things I really miss." He clutches a copy of the *International Herald-Tribune*. "This is a great paper, but I'd like to read an American newspaper, turn on a baseball game. Americanisms, I guess you'd call them. Vic Dickenson's right, I guess. I ran into Vic at a festival and he said, 'Listen, Bud, it's time you came back. The word's around.'"

Briskly strolling though Hyde Park, Freeman obviously enjoys his daily excursions around London. He is suddenly reminded of Charlie Parker. "There's no question he was a genius of the saxophone. He just didn't take care of his health and that's very important. It was only fairly recently that I sat down and listened to all of his recordings." Other favorites? "Well, there's always a problem of leaving someone out, but certainly Bix, Louis [Armstrong], and King Oliver. What can you say? Stan Getz, I love. He's certainly the best of the modern tenor players and I also had great respect for John Coltrane. A tragedy he died so young. And Dave Tough had to have been one of the greatest drummers. Just ask Max Roach about him. Then there's this youngster, Scotty Hamilton. He played in England when I was here. I find it incredible that he went toward Ben Webster rather than Parker. I hear that in his playing, although he's certainly his own man."

Freeman described his own playing with characteristic honesty. "I play pretty much the same style, with a better sound possibly, better beat, better knowledge of harmonic and melodic lines, but I still practice about an hour a day, creative things I hope to incorporate in my playing. I still find music all very exciting. Through the years I've learned to get rid of a lot of the rubbish I played, and I'm tending more toward melodic lines. I like to play ballads more than I did, but with a definite beat. I'd love to see people dancing again."

He starts toward his hotel. There's packing to do, a call from his agent about yet another job. "I guess you could say," he says, stopping to make a point, "I just love playing the horn."

—London and Chicago, 1980–81

Two

The Modern Exiles

5

The Modern Exiles

As the war raged on in Europe, a musical revolution, spearheaded by the standard-bearers of bebop, was taking place on New York's 52nd Street. Charlie Parker, Dizzy Gillespie, and Thelonious Monk led a brigade of experimenters who sought to free themselves from the confines of the big swing bands and into the more adventuresome harmonic and rhythmic complexities of what would become known as bebop. In Europe, the boom in traditional jazz continued, but even in America the new developments in jazz were obscured by an additional factor.

A recording ban, which went into effect on August 1, 1942, and lasted until the fall of 1944, prevented anything like a mass audience from hearing the bands of Earl "Fatha" Hines, singer-trumpeter Billy Eckstine—both of whom employed a number of bebop musicians— or the small groups of Gillespie and Parker.

By 1945, bebop was firmly entrenched, and its effects were already causing reverberations in the big dance bands that had been the mainstay of the swing era. The bebop innovators injected their own ideas into the big band format and forged an entirely new music.

In addition to Gillespie, Parker, and Miles Davis, pianists Bud Powell and George Wallington, bassist Oscar Pettiford, and drummers Max Roach and Kenny Clarke all sought and found new outlets for a new music. Pianist Tadd Dameron would emerge as the most important arranger of this period. Of these key musicians, four would become exiles.

Although there were a number of holdouts from the more traditional forms of jazz, many of the leading swing players found themselves working alongside the beboppers in the clubs that dotted 52nd Street. Coleman Hawkins and Lester Young were two such musicians, but it was tenor saxophonist Don Byas who was regarded as the best to bridge the gap between swing and bebop. For Byas, 52nd Street proved to be only a brief stopover on the road to Europe, where he would become the first important modern exile.

Byas had come to New York with Eddie Mallory's band in 1937. He remained for eighteen months before brief stints with Don Redman, Lucky Millinder, and Andy Kirk. In 1941, Byas joined the Count Basie Band. When he got off the bus in 1943, he began to work with Gillespie, a number of all-star groups, and several small bands under his own name.

Byas's playing was much in the vein of Coleman Hawkins, and the early records with Gillespie clearly show Byas was at home with the demands of the new music. His already melodic lines were further enriched by the influence of Parker and his disciples. With the lifting of the recording ban, Byas recorded for several of the new, small jazz labels that were springing up everywhere. He even had a minor hit with his own version of "Laura" in 1946. The same year, he garnered first place honors in the *Esquire* jazz poll.

But Byas was restless, and when Don Redman formed another band, Byas joined him for an extended European tour. When the tour ended, Byas stayed on in Europe to have a look around. He was still looking around a quarter of a century later. He was not seen or heard in the States again until 1970 when he appeared at the Newport Jazz Festival. His Newport appearance was to be the final scene in a documentary film on his life in jazz, produced by a Dutch production company.

As the first of the postwar exiles, Byas became a guiding figure in the careers of the many musicians who would follow in his footsteps. Living first in France, Byas later settled permanently in Holland and was regularly featured at jazz festivals throughout Europe as a soloist with visiting bands such as Duke Ellington, or with Norman Granz's Jazz at the Philharmonic tours with Coleman Hawkins and Stan Getz.

While in Europe, Byas took up skin diving and deep-sea fishing and became something of a physical fitness buff. He had left a drinking problem behind, which was one of the principal reasons he had left the States, but eventually encountered the hazards many of the exiles experienced. His stay in Europe was so lengthy that he began to be taken for granted and was considered a "local" by many promoters and club owners. The mushrooming number of exiles that followed Byas's lead made working conditions difficult and bruised his fierce ego. He began to drink heavily again and his physical condition deteriorated. Finally, he became almost inactive, playing only sporadically, but often losing jobs to other Americans who ironically had come to Europe after him.

Lucky Thompson (Ken Whitten Collection)

At one point, Byas considered going home. "I may do that," he said. "One more trip, one grand tour. I'll make some money, come back, and then I'll lie down and die."[1] He returned to the States for the 1970 Newport appearance and toured Japan with Art Blakey's Jazz Messengers in 1971. He returned to Holland the following year and at age fifty-nine died of cancer.

In addition to his many musical achievements, Byas's success in Europe encouraged many other musicians to follow his lead. Herbert "Peanuts" Holland was a section mate of Byas in the Don Redman tour of 1946. Like Byas, Holland stayed in Europe after the tour. He had previously worked with Fletcher Henderson and Charlie Barnet, and though not of the stature of Byas, Holland continued to work in Europe as a touring soloist for a number of years.

Following close on the heels of Byas and Holland was clarinetist Milton "Mezz" Mezzrow. After visiting France periodically from 1929, Mezzrow settled in France in 1948. He is also credited with introducing French critic Hugues Panassie to the records of Louis Armstrong, an event that led to the formation of the Hot Club of France.

When commenting on the jazz exiles, Mezzrow said, "Most of the Negroes who are here aren't here because of the race question. It's just that you can live your life the way you wish and nobody bothers you . . . people treat you as an artist, not the way they treat jazz musicians in the States."[2]

Although not a brilliant technician, Mezzrow was considered a fine blues player. He was also the author of *Really the Blues*, published in France in 1946. The book became a best-seller and recounts Mezzrow's many adventures in jazz and his close association with black musicians. His identification with blacks was so intense, he was often called the first "white Negro." From 1948 until his death in 1972, Mezzrow remained in Europe, returning home only for brief visits.

■■■■ The Bebop Invasion of Europe

When Dizzy Gillespie toured Europe with his bebop big band in 1948, the impact on audiences and musicians alike was immense. The tour marked the birth of bebop in France. One of the principal reasons for the band's success was the solo work of tenor saxophonist James Moody, who was featured on several arrangements.

But if the musical pace of the band was fierce, so was the living. Eventually it caught up with Moody. He left the band and went to

Paris to stay with relatives for much-needed rest and recuperation from the rigors of the road. "I went for a little while and stayed three years," says Moody. "The place was beautiful, in a nice neighborhood near the Eiffel Tower. I wasn't going home at all until Babs Gonzales came over to tell me I had a hit record."[3]

The hit was a variation on "I'm in the Mood for Love." Moody had recorded it in Sweden on a borrowed horn and in one of those strange quirks of fate, it eventually made its way to Prestige Records and hit the juke boxes throughout America. Moody returned home a minor star in 1951. After a falling out with singer Gonzales, Moody replaced him with Eddie Jefferson, who, according to Moody, is the rightful author of "Moody's Mood." The lyrics written in substitution for the saxophone solo are often erroneously attributed to another vocalist, King Pleasure, who "borrowed" the lyrics from Jefferson.

In 1963, Moody was reunited with Dizzy Gillespie for an association that lasted eight years. Then, following periods of fronting his own small groups, Moody landed in the most unlikely place for a jazz musician: the house band of the Hilton Hotel in Las Vegas. Moody stayed seven years, although he originally planned to pursue a career in the Hollywood studios. But the lure of jazz was too strong, and with the exception of the late Monk Montgomery's efforts with the Las Vegas Jazz Society, and Alan Grant's Monday Night Jazz at the Four Queens Hotel, there were few opportunities for jazz in this desert community.

Moody returned to New York to appear at a welcome-home concert at Town Hall. The capacity crowds put him back on the jazz trail once again. It is ironic, though, that a record made in Sweden while Moody was living in Paris was the catalyst that ended his period of exile and brought him back to America.

■■■ Tadd Dameron

Another contemporary of Moody's was Tadd Dameron, whose piano playing was far overshadowed by his arranging and composing talents. Dameron had gone to Paris with trumpeter Miles Davis for the Paris Jazz Festival but then remained abroad for three years, returning to America in 1951. Two of the three years were spent in England. As with Benny Carter ten years earlier, it was Dameron's arranging skills that kept him busy.

He wrote for the British bands of Ted Heath and Vic Lewis as well as for a number of bands on the Continent. English musicians, however, bemoaned the fact that Dameron was not heard enough. His impact on modern jazz in Great Britain was not nearly what it might have been.

Typically, Dameron had gone largely unrecognized in America. Considered *the* arranger of the forties, Dameron was best at translating complex bebop lines to the big band format, although his first love was composing. He penned several standards—"Our Delight," "Good Bait," "Lady Bird"—which became staples of the bebop repertoire and were written by Dameron at age twenty-two.

Although not a great soloist, Dameron could accompany with the best pianists, and often played with the 52nd Street crowd while continuing to arrange for Benny Carter, Teddy Hill, and Gillespie. In 1947, Dameron won the *Esquire* jazz critics poll in the category of new star arranger. With the promotion of Monte Kay—a vital force in promoting modern jazz—Dameron assumed the house band leadership at the Royal Roost. The job lasted thirty-nine weeks, ironically during a period when other jazz clubs were struggling. The Roost engagement featured many of the premier players of bebop and further established Dameron as a force to be reckoned with.

Dameron later contributed compositions to the Clifford Brown–Max Roach band, and he is credited with being the first to discover the prodigious talents of trumpeter Brown. One of his compositions, "Fontainebleau," an impressionistic piece penned from his memories of France, drew the attention of British conductor Sir Thomas Beecham, who later recorded the piece. Unfortunately, it was never released.

Dameron continued to arrange for a wide variety of artists through the early sixties—Milt Jackson, Blue Mitchell, Tony Bennett, Sarah Vaughan—praised by all but often neglected until his death in 1964. Dameron's influence is perhaps best compared to arranger Gil Evans and his many collaborations with Miles Davis.[4]

Chet Baker (Ken Whitten Collection)

Chet Baker

In the mid-fifties, trumpeter Chet Baker left for an ill-fated tour of Europe that would eventually lead to an eighteen-month sentence in an Italian jail, the result of many bouts with a narcotics problem.

Baker came to national prominence in 1952 when he teamed with baritone saxophonist Gerry Mulligan for a series of recordings in a pianoless quartet. The group showcased Baker's Miles-like playing and placed him in the vanguard of the so-called West Coast sound. He was also singled out by Charlie Parker when he was on the West Coast for several engagements. But success seemed, for Baker, as hard to handle as his drug problem.

In a *Time* magazine interview in Paris, Baker said: "I left America because I had a medical problem—drugs. The Europeans treat drug addicts as sick, not as criminals, and I'm not going back home until I'm sure I'm all right."[5]

But Baker was arrested in Italy in 1961, and following his eighteen-month prison sentence, he was deported. Arrested again in Munich in 1963 Baker was told to stay out of Germany for three years. He returned shortly, however, and was arrested again in Berlin, where he spent forty days in a hospital. He worked the Blue Note in Paris for several months and then was offered a movie in England, but trouble found him again and once more he was deported. Baker truly seemed to have worn out his welcome in Europe.

Writer Ira Gitler asked Baker why, when there were several other musician addicts in Europe, a pattern of harassment seemed to follow him. "I don't know," Baker said. "It just seemed like a field day for the police department whenever Chet Baker came to town. It seemed to be a tie-up between the police department and the newspapers— the publicity bit—because I was always very cool, I never bothered anybody. I never sold drugs to anybody. Everything I did was for myself."[6]

Time magazine reported that his homecoming in April 1964 left him with $1.25 in his pocket and few friends. A short time later, he played for New York audiences for the first time in five years with a pickup rhythm section at a Long Island club. The *Time* reviewer said, "He looked pained when he played and downright wounded when he sang, but his music had a bright aggressive gusto to it that made better jazz than the music his fans remembered. Having marinated his art in misery, he seemed at last on a better road than the one he lost."[7]

Returning home, however, wasn't such a good choice. Although he claimed to be reformed, he slipped again and was beset by exploitive employers who took advantage of his previous reputation. Finally, one night in 1968, on the way home from work in San Francisco, Baker was robbed and severely beaten. Struggling once again on the comeback trail, he managed to bounce back, and by the mid-seventies he was reunited with Gerry Mulligan and began to record again under his own name.

In the seventies, Baker spent more and more time in Europe, recording quite often, and completed a video that included playing and a relaxed interview conducted by bassist Red Mitchell in Sweden. He also took part in the 1986 film 'Round Midnight, recording several songs for the sound track album.

There is also a video, filmed at Ronnie Scott's club in London shortly before his death. In it, Baker is frail, working without a drummer and clumsily and inexplicably joined by British singers Elvis Costello and Van Morrison. The unique Baker vocals are there, as are the hornlike scat singing and, of course, the vibratoless trumpet. Some of his playing recalls the Baker of old.

His death, at age fifty-nine, on May 13, 1988, in Holland remains shrouded in mystery. He fell from a second-story window, and suicide was suggested; but as Ira Gitler says, "You don't commit suicide by going out a second-floor window."[8]

▬▬ Kenny Clarke

In 1956, a year after Baker's departure to Europe, the man who changed the course of jazz drumming and helped found one of the most famous groups in jazz, the Modern Jazz Quartet, left for France. Kenny "Klook" Clarke never lived in the States again.

It was Clarke's drums that sparked Dizzy Gillespie's band when it toured Europe in 1948 and made him a favorite with French fans and critics alike. That first European experience also set the stage for Clarke's decision to live permanently in France. After the tour with Gillespie's band, Clarke returned to tour a number of times for extensive periods. Back in New York in 1951, he toured with Billy Eckstine and became a member of a quartet with Milt Jackson, Percy Heath, and Horace Silver. When Silver left, John Lewis replaced him and the MJQ was born. Lewis, however, took the group in a different direction, a less swinging one, Clarke felt. So much so that he left and was replaced by Connie Kay, the group's drummer for the duration.

By 1956, Clarke was restless, disillusioned with New York, and disappointed in the jazz scene. Charlie Parker was dead, the drug scene was pervasive, and Clarke was disgusted with record companies paying musicians at times in narcotics. The musicians were being taken advantage of by promoters, some of whom Clarke confronted when he discovered even Dizzy Gillespie was one of their targets. The promoters threatened Clarke with blackballing but he refused to give in. He was also haunted by memory of his European success. He was

Kenny "Klook" Clarke (Ken Whitten Collection)

still a favorite of the French. Why not go where jazz was appreciated? When opportunity knocked, Clarke threw open the door.

Michel Legrand offered Clarke a two-year contract in a big band his uncle, Jacques Helian, was forming. Arriving in France, Clarke found he was still very well remembered from earlier tours. Although the Helian band broke up, Clarke had plenty of offers to stay. The jazz clubs on the Left Bank, film and television studios, and concert halls became the domain for Clarke and his drums. When he wasn't leading groups at the Blue Note or Club St. Germain des Pres, he was touring Europe and doing, perhaps, better than he could have in New York.

Dizzy Gillespie had no doubts. "I don't *think* Kenny is doing better in Europe than he would be over here. I *know* so." Despite being in Europe, Clarke felt not the least bit cut off from American friends. Dizzy and many musicians came through Paris on a regular basis.

Clarke's success continued into the sixties. In 1961 he formed a big band with Belgian pianist Francy Boland and promoter Gigi Campi.

The band was a mix of European musicians and American exiles such as Nathan Davis, Johnny Griffin, Benny Bailey, Kenny Drew, Nat Peck, Jimmy Woode, and Sahib Shihab. The band toured and recorded extensively, once, ironically for the U.S. State Department. In the band's eleven years they recorded thirty-seven albums and were often promoted as a proof of jazz's universal message.

If there was a damper on this scene for Clarke, it was the attempt by the French musicians' union to establish a quota system for foreign musicians working in Paris, similar to the one that already existed in England. One or two foreign headliners—Clarke was one of these—would be permitted to continue playing clubs, but lesser-known Americans would be replaced or barred entirely.

The campaign touched off a major controversy in French music circles. The American musicians had become, in the words of one journalist, "the most productive group since the 'lost generation' of American writers—Hemingway, Fitzgerald, Pound." Union leaders Michel Hausser and Gil Lafite claimed they represented some fifty French musicians. Their campaign was based on a 1933 law that said foreigners must not represent more than 10 percent of a night spot band. The law also, however, provided for exceptions that allowed that number to increase to 30 percent.

When told he would have to replace Nathan Davis in the Clarke–Lou Bennet group, Blue Note manager Ben Benjamin said, "The fact that I have to change just him [Davis] alone is going to lower the standards of the club."

Other clubs and Americans felt similar drafts. At the Living Room, American pianist Art Simmons worked with two Frenchmen, but the intermission pianist, Aaron Bridges, was a possible casualty of the union campaign.[9]

Despite extreme opposition, the union succeeded to a degree, although Clarke's position was never in question. Still, when he worked clubs like the Blue Note, the remaining members of the group were officially supposed to be French, but the policy was never strictly enforced.

Clarke remained in France until his death in 1988, continuing to work clubs and touring extensively. His long presence in Europe also made him something of an elder statesman for the increasing numbers of jazz exiles making the Atlantic crossing. But as Ursula Davis points out, "It is ironic that Kenny had to leave a black jazz group [MJQ] and the cradle of black music to go to Europe to play the music he loved—the music that 'swings.'"

Stan Getz

Clarke was closely followed by saxophonists Lee Konitz and Lucky Thompson; violinist Stuff Smith; pianist Bud Powell; and in 1958, saxophonist Stan Getz. For Getz, moving to Europe was not a question of finding work in jazz. He was already critically and commercially successful. His best years were yet to come when he settled in Denmark with his Swedish wife, Monica, and four children.

"I'm tired of competition," Getz said. "I'm tired of tearing around making money. There are other things in life than making money. Here, I have more time with my family. I don't make as much money as in the States, but it's cheaper to live here. And it's unhurried. I enjoy the relaxed way of living in Europe. I wanted to find peace of mind. That's hard to find in the States."

Getz brought his Cadillac with him—which he quickly traded in—took up residence in a large home that he rented from a university professor, and made his headquarters the Montmartre, a dark, smoky club, lit by candles and furnished with long wooden tables. The house rhythm section often included Oscar Pettiford and Kenny Drew, and the relaxed atmosphere of Copenhagen gave Getz the opportunity to play and develop without pressure. "I like this life," he said. "It's a good life."

The life from which Getz had fled included a failed marriage, a long battle with heroin addiction, which culminated in an abortive drugstore holdup in Seattle, and a stint in the Los Angeles County Jail. He had threatened the clerk, but a customer, realizing he was only faking a gun, caused him to flee the store. Later he called to apologize for the crazy stunt, but the call was traced and Getz was arrested in

Stan Getz (Ken Whitten Collection)

his hotel. At the police station, he attempted suicide by swallowing a handful of sleeping pills.

"When I came out of the coma five days later I found a breathing tube inserted in my trachea. I had taken a lethal dose but the doctors saved me," said Getz. Two years later, he contracted pneumonia. His recovery was rapid but not complete. One of his lungs was damaged. Doctors suggested lots of outdoor exercise and no blowing. Convalescence near Mombassa on Africa's coast with Monica followed, and the two were married in Las Vegas in November 1956.

Returning to playing, Getz made the round of concerts, clubs, and tours and finally got off the merry-go-round in 1958. He continued to dominate the jazz polls and literally put Denmark on the jazz map. But by the time of his return to America in 1961, Sonny Rollins and John Coltrane were threatening his dominance on tenor. Getz's response was to team up with Eddie Sauter for the *Focus* recording sessions, and the following year he collaborated with guitarist Charlie Byrd to launch the bossa nova craze with their *Jazz Samba* album that included "One Note Samba" and "Desafinado." Getz later knocked the Beatles off the charts with "Girl from Ipanema."

Retreating from success and the wave of avant garde jazz, Getz returned to Europe again in 1969, this time to Spain. He worked all over the Continent, touring and recording, and eventually moving into his next phase with pianist Chick Corea, recording *Captain Marvel* and *Sweet Rain*, musts in the Getz collection.

Getz felt, as did Phil Woods, that much more could be done to further the cause of jazz. "It's ironic how little we do to help our own. Did you know that in Denmark all the jazz clubs are subsidized? When I play over there in small towns where they may lose money, the government picks up the slack. No wonder so many of our best and brightest had to seek haven in Europe in order to survive.

"Too many great men have been lost to early deaths—they were burned out by the continuous travel, the drain of creating when there was little regard for what they did. Why did a marvelous saxophonist like Ben Webster have to waste his last years in Europe when his value as a teacher could have been put to such great use in some of our schools?"

Getz's final years were anything but wasted and, ironically, two of his last recordings, *Anniversary* and *Serenity*, regarded as among his best, were done in Denmark, once again at the Montmartre in Copenhagen.

■■■ Johnny Griffin

Johnny Griffin, like Eddie "Lockjaw" Davis, his one-time partner in a group, began playing in the forties. Another of the hard-swinging tenors, Griffin came to New York and joined Art Blakey's Jazz Messengers in 1957, was with Thelonious Monk from 1958 to 1960, and formed a group with "Jaws" [Eddie Davis] that continued through 1962. A brief trip to Europe in December of that year proved to be a revelation for the man often called "Little Giant."

"I had an awakening," Griffin said. "The way people treated black

Johnny Griffin

musicians—or jazz musicians in general—was comparable to the respect they accord to classical artists. Coming back to New York, I ran
into the same old hassles; the musicians standing around at Beefsteak
Charlie's complaining about booking agents and record companies. I
didn't need this anymore. I'd enjoyed a period of relaxation and felt I
could have a more dignified life in Europe, so I took off in the summer
of 1963." [10]

Griffin lived in Paris for ten years before moving to a little village called Berhambacht, not far from Rotterdam. "Paris was fine, except that living in an apartment was driving me crazy." Now, Griffin says, "I just go out and make my gigs, then go back to this five-hundred-year-old village and relax, compose, blow my horn, tend my garden. It's a life I couldn't live over here [America]."

If he missed anything being away from America, it was, as many of the exiles have said, family—Griffin hadn't seen his kids for fifteen years—and the musicians, although Griffin works regularly with fellow exiles. "I miss delivery services. You know, sending out for food and other things. Americans do everything fast. At first, I was climbing the walls in Europe. I'd call the desk clerk in a hotel and he'd be out to lunch. The French people would says, 'Calm down. Have some lunch.' I never learned how to relax until I went to Europe.[11] Otherwise, I don't miss nothin'. Except the sports. I miss baseball, football, though I've gotten interested in soccer."

On his first visit home in 1978, Griffin found, however, that he also missed the reaction of American audiences. Dexter Gordon's return in 1976 had opened the door for returning exiles and Griffin found the experience overwhelming.

"I had forgotten how well American audiences could react. Americans can relate to it because it's part of our own culture, yet on the whole they tend to hear things a little more superficially. In Europe the people are taught to accept any and all art forms, to really study and learn to appreciate them. They are magnetized by jazz; it's the strong life force in the music that grabs them. They will tell you things about yourself that you didn't know. They like the music, they like the sound, but they don't really know what I'm blowing about. I've come to the conclusion that they like this feeling of swing because it's so foreign to their culture; there's such a strong life force in the music that it overwhelms them. But, then, they can take it for granted like the American public has done.[12]

"Now don't get me wrong. Europeans really appreciate the music. But Americans are more spontaneous. I can feel the thirst for the music when I walk out on stage. Americans talk to the musicians while they're playing. They encourage them to play harder. And the musicians respond. It's fun playing for Americans."

Today, Griffin continues to make trips home for tours and recordings, but, like Art Farmer, he has no immediate plans to make his home anywhere but Europe. He is troubled also by the commercialization of many jazz musicians. "It hurts me to see so many young musicians, even some of the older ones, sacrificing their talents when the record companies wave that big buck in front of their faces. The producers are trying to poison their souls, and there is not even any guarantee of success, especially if they can't play that commercial stuff sincerely.

"The powers that be want to change the music into something else so that everyone can play it and make it common. The music that I play is not common. It is not meant for the masses in the first place. It's not ever supposed to be popular like rock and I never expected it would be, wouldn't care if it ever was. Jazz is creativity. We can't make jazz a commodity that you can sell in the supermarket. Jazz is not for everybody. Only a few special people are attuned to this music, but they're scattered all over this planet."[13] For Griffin, Europe seems to have more of these special people.

Getz, Gordon, Griffin, and other new members of the exiles' club signaled the first reverberations of a wave of jazz exiles that would swell to dramatic proportions during the sixties. By the time the four young men from Liverpool arrived on the American scene, the die was cast. Rock music burst on the marketplace with a force that would have a lasting effect on jazz. The search for artistic development and acceptance continued to be a dominating factor in the exile movement as jazz was crowded off the stage by the proliferation of rock bands. But the additional issues of race, politics, and the Vietnam War would come into play as the exodus continued and involved all styles of jazz and a host of major names.

By the end of the sixties, Phil Woods, Mal Waldron, Slide Hampton, Philly Joe Jones, Art Taylor, Dave Pike, Ben Webster, Maynard Ferguson, Red Mitchell, Leo Wright, Carmel Jones, and singers Mark Murphy and Jon Hendricks would follow the trail blazed by Sidney Bechet, Don Byas, and Kenny Clarke. The New York maelstrom was abandoned for London, Paris, Stockholm, and Copenhagen.

These musicians would be joined by the leading exponents of

the free jazz movement—Cecil Taylor, Burton Greene, Ornette Coleman—as well as by Chicagoan Bud Freeman, former Oscar Peterson drummer Ed Thigpen, and arrangers Ernie Wilkins and Thad Jones.

Many would return to enjoy the fruits of their European exile and go on to successful careers in the country that had given birth to their music but had largely neglected its artists.

6

*I knew I was doing
something I would
treasure for the rest
of my life.
— Jay Cameron*

Jay Cameron

Saxophonist Jay Cameron arrived in Paris early enough to remember witnessing jam sessions with Django Reinhardt. Cameron and a friend originally were headed for a music conservatory in Lausanne, Switzerland. "We wanted to study oboe," Cameron says, "and I wanted to see if it was possible to study there on the G.I. Bill. We only stayed about six months though when we realized all the action was in Paris."

Those early years—Cameron went over in 1947—are fondly remembered. Besides Django, Cameron recalls Don Byas, traveling up from Spain, and refusing to speak anything but Spanish; the Paris appearances of Roy Eldridge, Coleman Hawkins; and spending time with the musicians in Paris on the Jazz at the Philharmonic tours, which then included Lester Young and Max Roach.

"I knew Max from New York," says Cameron, "so I never missed a chance to hang out with him and Prez. He [Lester Young] was so funny that by the end of the day the corners of my mouth would hurt from laughing so much."

Cameron had studied French in high school, so he quickly adapted to the language and the French people. "At that time, I could make it. I spent the summer of forty-nine in Monte Carlo, doing gigs for rich people at various functions. I felt like I was kind of making the jet set scene with no money, and living in Paris was so inexpensive at that time. I didn't really miss anything about the States. I was sick of being poor, but my feeling was that by being an American in these different situations, I knew I was doing something that I would treasure for the rest of my life."

During much of 1950, Cameron worked in Belgium with some of the best Belgian musicians; among them was pianist Francy Boland, who would later form a big band with Kenny Clarke. By the end of the year, however, Cameron thought maybe it was time to go home.

"It wasn't good. I came back to New York in 1951. I ended up working a day job and rehearsing with one of Gerry Mulligan's first big bands. I was playing alto then, but there was no work. As soon as I could get the money together, I headed back to Paris."

Returning to Paris, Cameron met other musicians and started to become a part of the Paris jazz scene. "Things began to get better as I got involved with Jimmy Gourley, a guitarist who is still there today. I did some recording for Swing Records with people like Barney Wilen, who I think was about seventeen at the time, and Bobby Jaspar. We got to do some touring. Bob Dorough was there then too. I'd gotten to know him in New York. I didn't see much of him. He was doing a single on the Right Bank; I was in the caves on the Left."

Cameron worked in Paris and other venues throughout Europe off and on for nearly seven years, but in 1955 he decided it really was time to go back to New York. "I thought about L.A. but I got a whole different message from Al Cohn and Zoot [Sims] and instead, joined Woody's band for the best part of a year." When the Herman band was booked into Las Vegas, it was with a smaller group, so Cameron returned to New York.

He found an apartment on the Lower East side in what could only be called a jazz neighborhood. There were jam sessions at organist Larry Rivers's loft; Elvin Jones and Pepper Adams were sharing an apartment nearby; Jimmy Garrison, Lee Morgan, and Ted Curson were all neighbors, as was a struggling young singer who had decided writing lyrics to jazz solos was a good idea.

"Jon Hendricks was driving me crazy with Basie tunes. He lived next door, and he would play these Basie records over and over trying to write lyrics for them," Cameron laughs.

Cameron stuck it out in New York, working with the bands of Maynard Ferguson and Dizzy Gillespie, and later he made one return trip to Paris with trombonist Slide Hampton in 1963. His last foreign tour was with saxophonist Paul Winter to South America.

In 1965, married and beginning a family, Cameron moved to the Pocono Mountains, an hour and a half from New York City. During this period, he owned a music store and even tried his hand at running a jazz club called The Lone Pine.

"It was a dream," Cameron says. "Musically, it was great. I got a lot of people to come up there from New York. Sal Nistico, Jon Eardley, George Coleman, Eddie Daniels, Steve Gilmore, Bill Goodwin, and sometimes Keith Jarrett, but he would only play drums then. It was just hard to make it go."

Leaving The Lone Pine behind, Cameron decided to move further west. His intention was again to explore opportunities in Los Angeles and San Francisco but he got no further than Las Vegas. "My mother was living here and there was quite a scene then, a lot of rehearsal bands going on. Shortly after I arrived, I went into the Tropicana for two and a half years with the *Folies Bergere* show."

For his first love, Cameron joined the community of jazz players who had either settled permanently in Las Vegas or spent considerable time there. Trombonist Carl Fontana and saxophonist Eddie "Lockjaw" Davis were already there, as were Garvin Bushell and bassist Carson Smith. James Moody would do a stint in the Hilton house band; Don Menza was yet to arrive for an artist-in-residence position at the University of Nevada, Las Vegas.

It was during this period that Cameron got very involved with another jazz resident, bassist Monk Montgomery. The brother of guitarist Wes, Monk Montgomery had settled in Las Vegas and was running the Las Vegas Jazz Society. Montgomery's efforts at staging concerts, jazz picnics, and keeping the jazz message alive rubbed off on Cameron. He began his role as desert jazz crusader. But despite the pool of jazz talent available, jazz was as tough a sell as it had been in the Pocono Mountains.

"It takes a certain turn of mind to be involved with jazz and it just isn't here," Cameron says of Las Vegas, although he continues to remain optimistic despite the difficulties.

In the eighties Cameron began working at a converted country and western club called the Hobnob. It truly is across the tracks, light years away from the Las Vegas Strip. There are still huge blowups of Dolly Parton, Kenny Rogers, and Willie Nelson, holdovers from the club's country music days. It's now a heavy metal venue on weekends, but Tuesday and Wednesday nights were devoted to jazz until early 1992, when new ownership decided against the jazz policy.

For nearly seven years the club was a haven where musicians could stop by and sit in after performing for Strip hotel shows. For the hardcore local jazz fans, the Hobnob became a hangout. Cameron played there often and also booked other local bands. The pay was poor—the musicians took only a percentage of the bar—but it was a place to play, try out new arrangements, and as Cameron says, "keep up your chops." With the exception of former New York DJ Alan Grant's Monday Night Jazz at the Four Queens Hotel, the Hobnob was the only other regular jazz game in town.

With years to reflect on his European experience Cameron says now of Paris, "I was probably a little bigger fish in a little smaller pond. Jimmy Gourley was very influential for me, studying harmony with him. Rhythm sections were always a problem then. Horn players learned from the records; rhythm section players, especially drummers, needed to see how it was done by American drummers."

Cameron was also made aware of the attitude of local musicians in Paris. The exception was the Left Bank clubs, but being an American in Paris was not always easy going. "French musicians resented American musicians taking jobs, except on the jazz scene. There was not much difference. Nat Peck [trombonist] was there a long time. He became very French and managed to break in the legit scene. I felt comfortable living there. I was right down on the level with the people. The JATP [Jazz at the Philharmonic] cats really didn't see anything of the real Paris."

Of the French jazz fans, Cameron has mixed feelings. "I haven't been over there since sixty-three, with Slide Hampton, but it seems to me that the Americanization of Europe has led to the same thing that we have here. French people have been brought up on rock just like here. Control of the media is the same now. The simpler music is, the quicker it'll move through the system, and these businessmen have found this out. The music that they've instilled—bullshit and lack of substance—the main thing in Europe is that they have more respect for culture. So when they see it [jazz], they recognize it as culture, a melting pot music. Jazz is one of the best reflections of this.

"However, the rest of the general public is as far from understanding it as they are in America. Those few people who have been exposed to it between the ages of ten and twenty get turned on to jazz. That's where jazz fans are at today. Education is the key. All of us who were in the music just assumed because it had so much to offer that everyone would pick up on it. Today we're still reeling in astonishment. What happened? When I had the music store, I saw that if my customers had been exposed to jazz early they would get into it."

In the bins of record stores today musicians such as David Sanborn and Kenny G, both self-admitted nonjazz players who nevertheless carry the jazz label, are found alongside Dizzy Gillespie, Miles Davis, and Oscar Peterson. Cameron, however, sees this as not such a bad thing. "The person who latches on to what they're doing has already been exposed to rock, enough so that Kenny appeals. People just don't know about these things. They might have been real jazz fans. The more that's around, the more they think that's what's happening in jazz." But, like Lockjaw Davis, Cameron feels recordings of the jazz greats will tell the final story. "Recording reveals the substance of these musicians. Someday, somebody will listen to their records and realize what they were doing."

Today Cameron continues his jazz crusade, dividing his time between money-making gigs at the Strip hotels and playing jazz whenever and wherever he can. In the fall of 1992, Cameron returned to Europe for an extended tour of Belgium and France and a reunion with some of his musical friends from the fifties. Because of the strike in 1990 and the changeover in many of the hotels from live music to tape, Cameron and other Las Vegas musicians are finding it more difficult to make ends meet. As a result, Cameron has turned his attention to education.

A video in which he talks about his life in jazz is, he hopes, an avenue to doing more colleges and school clinics, getting the jazz message across to young people. "That *is* the key," Cameron says. "I still say today if we started with five-year-olds, we'd have an audience for jazz."

Reflecting on his Paris experience today, Cameron still counts it as one of the most fruitful periods of his life. Immersing himself in French life, he came, like a number of other exiles, to know himself as an American.

"The Metro stopped running at midnight, so when we played a late gig somewhere, we'd have to wait for the first train at five in the morning. All these French people were going to work—we're all crammed in there together—but it seemed we were always taller so we could talk to each other over the heads of the Frenchmen. It seemed kind of symbolic to me. We had a certain attitude, developed a certain introspection, that made us take a closer look at ourselves. I enjoyed that, getting to know myself as an American in Paris. Travel, play some music, eventually I knew I'd have to settle down, but that was my feeling while I was over there."

—Las Vegas, 1991

7

Bob Dorough

Bob Dorough has several albums under his own name but it was perhaps a Christmas song recorded with Miles Davis that garnered him the most attention. "It was 1962. I'd been in L.A. for three years working with trios, a quintet. Miles became kind of a fan, heard my Bethlehem album *Devil May Care*, which I'd done in 1956, so he called me up and asked me to write a Christmas song. That was 'Blue Christmas.'"

It's a very different Christmas song, but then most everything Dorough does is unique. For example, when he arrived in Europe, it was not with a horn player, but with a boxer—Sugar Ray Robinson.

"I went over with Sugar because he was in show business for two years. I met him in a tap dance studio in New York where I was playing rehearsals and eventually became his musical director. That was in the fall of 1952. I met people like Earl Hines and Count Basie on tours and I was the only musician in his entourage.

"We all sailed to France because Ray was superstitious about flying. By then I was getting a little bored with the job, but I thought, if he's going to Paris, I want to go. In Paris we did a big show, and I was trying to lead all these French cats. They weren't so hip in those days."

The association with Robinson, however, led to Dorough's staying in France. "Somewhere along the way I got involved in the Mars Club on the Right Bank. It was kind of like an East Side New York club. Blossom [Dearie] had worked there, Bobby Short, Annie Ross. So the owner said, 'If you ever quit Sugar Ray you know you got a job.' I'd been singing already so I saw it as a great opportunity to play and sing, which was what I wanted to do."

With Robinson's departure, the opportunity came sooner than Dorough expected, but the end of one gig was the beginning of a career. "One evening Sugar called me and said, 'We're leaving Monday, I'm going back into the ring.' So I wound up working the Mars for five more months, which carried me into 1955."

While most of the jazz action was on the Left Bank, Dorough was content to work and develop his unique vocal style at the Mars Club. The club "was like a little bit of New York City. Maya Angelou, Truman Capote, the cast of *Porgy & Bess*, lots of celebrities used to hang out there. Everything was going on over on the Left Bank. I would see some of those cats, they would come over, but I wasn't really a part of the Blue Note scene. But all kinds of musicians would be around like Jay Cameron and Art Simmons, who also played opposite me and the Mars. We had no nights off, so you just went to work."

Eventually, however, Dorough tired of the Right Bank scene and decided to go home. "I did get kind of homesick and blue for New York so I came home. I remember the date because it was just before Charlie Parker died in March of 1955."

Since 1981, Dorough has been making regular tours of Europe, often with his longtime friend and bassist Bill Takas. "I've been back a couple of times since I became a vocal jazz artist, but it was 1981 before I went back to work. I go for tours now, with Paris as headquarters. Sometimes they give us a drummer because a duo was a little too subtle for the French. I do Italy, Switzerland, Belgium, Norway, Sweden, and England. On the last tour I did six weeks."

There were, however, lean years that caused Dorough to turn his talents in other directions. "Yes, there were even years I couldn't work in the U.S. Jazz was sort of buried by rock 'n' roll, except for guys like Dizzy. My stuff just wasn't in vogue, so I got into producing."

Dorough turned his unusual talents with words to the world of education, and "Multiplication Rock," an ingenious combination of music and mathematics, proved to be a great success. Dorough also collaborated with another wordsmith-pianist-vocalist, Dave Frishberg. "I'm Hip" is a standard recorded by a number of vocalists.

Clever as many of Dorough's songs are, however, European audiences, as Jon Hendricks and Mark Murphy discovered, weren't always able to digest English lyrics. "It's better now," Dorough says, "but I had to slow down the tempo a bit. Like Prez [Lester Young] said, 'You gotta know the words.'"

Is jazz better received now in Europe? "I don't really think so. It's a big world and there are people in France who don't care about jazz. Before we knew it was art, I think the Europeans in their scholarly, distant view of it, saw it as an art form, accorded it a certain level Americans haven't gotten around to. Jazz fans tend to come and hear it. In a real jazz room, where the management cooperates with the artist and insists the audience come to listen, it's just as good at Kimball's [San Francisco] as in Paris."

Today Dorough lives in the Pocono Mountains and is a neighbor of Phil Woods. Dorough has no doubts about living in Europe again. "Every time I go over I think about it. I saw Richard Boone and Ernie Wilkins in Copenhagen recently, and, of course, like Bill Takas says, it just feels so good over there. I flirted with Paris but I didn't quite check in."

—June 1990

8

Art Farmer

Bob Dorough's latest recording features another of the jazz exiles, fluegelhornist Art Farmer. Like Phil Woods, Farmer made the Atlantic crossing in 1968. Vienna rather than Paris was his destination, however. Farmer had been to Europe several times in the early sixties. In 1965, he was asked by Viennese pianist Friedrich Gulda to be one of the judges for an international competition of young jazz musicians.

While in Vienna, Farmer heard about the formation of a radio jazz orchestra that needed a trumpet soloist. The job called for ten days a month, nine months a year. As Farmer describes it, his whole life had been lived for the possibility of playing jazz music. He decided to try it for a year; it worked out well. By 1968, he had given up his New York apartment, and since then, not living in New York hasn't mattered. "I'm a traveler, so it doesn't matter where I live," Farmer says. "My career is based on traveling so they [jazz fans] wouldn't see me more than once or twice a year if I was living in New York. They don't want to see anyone more than that."

Born in Council Bluffs, Iowa, Farmer and his brother Addison, a bassist who died suddenly in 1963, come from a family of doctors, lawyers, teachers, and ministers, all of whom played music. Growing up in Phoenix, Arizona, Farmer began on piano and violin, then took up trumpet after flirting with bugle, sousaphone, and cornet. He taught himself to read music and by age fifteen he was playing in a dance band that had in its book arrangements of Count Basie, Duke Ellington, and Jimmy Lunceford.

The two brothers later moved to Los Angeles, working in a cold-storage warehouse by day and meeting some of the jazz greats such as Hampton Hawes, Eric Dolphy, and Charlie Parker by night. Farmer remembers hearing Parker sit in once with a very poor piano player. Bird simply told him, "You take every opportunity you can."

Farmer made his first trip to New York with drummer Johnny Otis's big band. His playing, he admits, was forced then, and Otis let him go. A meeting with Freddy Webster, however, put him in the hands of Maurice Grupp. Farmer spent his days studying and practicing with Grupp and immersing himself in the clubs on 52nd Street by night. After a brief stay with Dizzy's big band, he left to tour with Jay McShann.

A lengthy stay with Lionel Hampton's band followed, a band that included Clifford Brown, Gigi Gryce, and Alan Dawson, and that led to Farmer's first trip to Europe in 1953. By the late sixties, Farmer had switched to the more mellow fluegelhorn after trying to get a similar sound from a trumpet.

At his home in Vienna, he practices four to five hours a day in a special sound-proof room. It's a home Farmer had built in one of the greenbelts near the Vienna Woods. Living conditions alone keep Farmer in Vienna. His son Georg is in a good school, and as Farmer says, "Vienna has an element of stability that I think has improved me as a musician."

At first, however, Farmer had to be content with getting used to things European—shop schedules, for example. "If you want to buy a car you can buy a car Sunday night, at least in California. That's an extreme example, but over there, everything closes at noon on Saturday."

When he first went over, he stayed as long as two or three years without returning to America. Because of the number of musicians coming over, Farmer didn't really miss the New York music scene. He studied and learned some German. "It's [language] not an obstacle but you try to learn as much and as soon as you can. Many people speak English in Vienna, but sometimes everyone is talking German around you."

When not traveling, Farmer lives a quiet, almost reclusive life at home in Vienna. "I live from the inside to the outside, not from the outside to the inside," Farmer says. He plays a few clubs in Vienna and works with local rhythm sections around the Continent and in England. Three or four times a year he travels back to the States for club dates, concerts, and recording and there have also been trips to Japan.

Despite over twenty years in Europe, Farmer feels the European jazz fan's acceptance is similar to an American's. "No difference at all. If you just go over there on a trip you might think so because you see people who are interested in jazz, but if you live there you meet people for whom jazz is not part of their lives at all. It varies, depends on the individual, the situation, the status of the person. With true fans, there is no difference. We welcome them but they [Americans] are more easily distracted than Europeans who really want to hear the music, are more quiet, have a purpose, concentrate on the music. Americans see an ad in the paper, go to the club and listen for a few minutes, then talk."

Farmer does agree with Phil Woods that America could use a Voice of America for Americans. "He's completely right. The lack of jazz appreciation is symbolic of the general state of affairs in the U.S., like many other things—economics, greed, prejudice—that bother the whole scene. People that have the power are only concerned with getting more power and money. Everything is based on money, the bottom line. Things that don't produce the bottom line, there's a tendency to go on to the next thing. If you don't show a profit, go on. Record companies' concern is how many and how fast can you sell. We're becoming the most illiterate country in the civilized world, something we're going to pay for down the road."

In recent years the music Farmer has always played has been designated "acoustic jazz." "It's just sales hype. It saddens me though when jazz is misused that way. People who are really trying to play jazz get shunted aside. When you reach sixty-one, you just do the best you can without worrying about things out of your control. I don't think about them. They do what they want to do."

Life in Vienna has been very good for Farmer. As he says, "I have not had a single bad racial experience since I've been in Europe. No one has been rude, no one has ignored me as people will do here [America] if they don't want to serve you or sell you a ticket. There has never been the slightest trouble with hotels or restaurants, although there is a slight surliness in the air in London.

"Sometimes people stare at you in remote Austrian towns, but they would stare at you the same way they would stare at a car they had never seen before. It's always something of a shock to come back here, because nothing has changed much. The same hangups are there. A person who plays jazz can go anywhere else in the world and never feel like a stranger. I can play the tiniest European town and be recognized. In an American town of the same size, or even in a good-sized American town, I would be unknown."[1]

Art Farmer continues to do what he wants to do despite months on the road every year, in America, Europe, and Japan. "I've been traveling all my life. I don't know anybody that likes the traveling after forty years; it's something you have to do to make a living."

—May 1990

*You come to Europe and try to
fit in with another society and that's
when you really find out you're an
American and you dig it.
— Mark Murphy*

Mark Murphy

"I was a little fed up with American agents, and I still didn't realize at the time that as a jazz vocalist, you really have to do it all yourself. Paris sounded like just the adventure I needed," says Mark Murphy.

The year was 1962, and President John F. Kennedy was sparring with the Soviet Union over the removal of missiles from Cuba. Frank Sinatra recorded with Count Basie and the jazz world was shaken by the free jazz of Ornette Coleman. Free jazz, new thing, avante garde, whatever the label, jazz was undergoing yet another revolution. The arrival of the Beatles was still two years off, but rock music was on the rise. All things considered, it was a shaky climate for jazz singers, that elite corps of vocalists who can count among its members Mark Murphy.

Paris turned out to be more than Murphy had bargained for. The show he had contracted for—scheduled to be written by Michel Legrand—was shelved when, according to Murphy, the woman in charge spent more time on wine than on the show. The project folded before it opened, and Murphy was left stranded in Europe.

Fred Burkenhardt came to the rescue with offers of recordings for the Phillips label in Holland. That was the beginning of several years' work with Dutch radio producer Joop de Roo, an association that for Murphy endures today. The Holland connection culminated in a seven-part series for television featuring the music of Broadway composers with the Dutch Metropole Orchestra. "That was certainly one of the high points of my career. I'm still trying to get the Harold Arlen segment on in the States."

Born in Syracuse, New York, Mark Murphy, like a number of other jazz singers, came from a musical family thoroughly steeped in church music. Raised in a Methodist congregation that did a lot of singing, Murphy began at an early age. "My mother and father met in the choir. My grandmother played the organ, and she was succeeded by my aunt, who still plays every Sunday. They had me singing at the age of four."

Murphy's talent blossomed and by 1957 he was recording for Decca Records, an association that was less than amicable, but more the fault of Decca than Murphy. "I must have been doing something right.

Those records didn't sell awfully well, but a lot of people still have them. Decca couldn't decide what to do with me. They went back and forth trying for compromise albums that there was really no market for. Jazz was a dirty word then in recording vocalists, but it's a good label now," says Murphy.

By 1962 Murphy was beginning to receive well-deserved recognition through a series of recordings that featured arrangements by, among others, Ralph Burns. Bookings at the Village Vanguard and the Village Gate in New York, and appearances on television shows like the short-lived *Jazz Scene USA*, seemed to assure Murphy's arrival as a new star. But things were still not quite falling into place.

"In a way," says Murphy, "I guess I was still trying to be a cabaret singer in a tuxedo, but singing the things I liked. It just didn't work." Bored, frustrated with the American scene, the Paris offer seemed the best choice.

Fred Burkenhardt also provided Murphy with the necessary contacts for additional work around the Continent and prompted him to settle in England with London as a home base. Murphy soon discovered that his earlier records enjoyed much better distribution in Europe than America. "Besides, living in London at that time was great, and so cheap. You could live like a king."

The London period led to several forays into acting in a number of documentaries for the BBC, a series of live recordings with the BBC orchestra, and periodic appearances at Ronnie Scott's jazz club and the numerous other pubs that feature jazz around Great Britain. It was a period of contentment and more than ample work opportunities. Thanks to the forces of American musicians already in Europe, and the many more who would follow, Murphy never felt cut off from the American jazz scene.

"No, not really, because in a sense, jazz had gone underground. A lot of musicians were already here and more were coming over all the time. Then there was the Vietnam War to digest. Jazz had really moved to Europe, and let's face it, it's an American music."

In the tradition of all great jazz singers, Murphy's voice is his instrument. His own indelible stamp is ever-present, be it in a ballad from a Broadway show, a jazz evergreen, or the blues. A Mark Murphy performance is always marked by a commanding stage presence and accented by his tall good looks and modish dress.

A demanding performer, he insists on a high level of performance from accompanists, a practice that often entails preparation and rehearsal beyond expectation. "The constant rehearsing is the one thing that drives me 'round the bend, but until I can afford my own trio, there's no other way."

Pickup rhythm sections can be a problem even with rehearsal but Murphy doesn't see it any differently than a horn player. "I've developed a discipline for that now. It's just something you have to expect. Working in Europe, I'd have to rate the musicians I've come in contact with from excellent to superb. But getting the right guys is always a problem. I did some work in Denmark where they have a marvelous appreciation for jazz, but the trio was pretty impossible. Good players, but not with each other at that time. If you can't get the right players at the right time for that cohesion that's so necessary, it just doesn't work. But that's true anywhere. I can't always get the guys I want in Cincinnati either."

There are, however, some problems unique to singers performing in Europe, particularly when, as with Murphy, subtlety is a keynote in the performance. "They appreciate jazz to a certain degree but they don't understand a lot of the subtleties of performers like myself or Jackie Cain or Roy Kral, for instance. It's much more of a problem for singers than horn players. I'm somewhat limited with audiences in Europe because of the language problem. I don't work in France. My singing depends a lot on nuance in the lyric and other subtleties I can't do with audiences that really don't understand English. So of course my best audience is in England or Holland, where English is understood by the majority of people."

This is one of several drawbacks, Murphy feels, to working in Europe, despite the proliferation of American musicians on the scene. "Living and working in Europe is nothing to be that envious of. There are certain situations, like Herb Geller in Hamburg or Leo Wright in Berlin have, working with state radio orchestras. Now we don't have that in America. But you also run into the European educational system with jazz fans. There is too much concern for disciplines and categories. They want a certain kind of jazz, and two world wars have not erased the class system in England. Try to get out of your category, whatever they think it is, and they treat you like a bad soprano in Milan. They boo. They booed Anita O'Day and me in Bremen and Jon Hendricks and Annie Ross when they appeared with Georgie Fame instead of doing their Lambert, Hendricks & Ross bit. Now that's just a lot of spoiled-brat nonsense. They don't even have jazz festivals there anymore because they couldn't control the audiences. Believe me, man, jazz fans can be dangerous."

Still the bad experiences are infrequent and judging from Murphy's early years in London, the Paris fiasco seems to have been a blessing in disguise. Murphy agrees. "Yeah, I started to get a lot of work around the Continent too, but until 1970 I really made my basic living by doing live recordings for the BBC. There was a union agreement that required so much live recording to offset the air play on radio. The BBC had a fantastic library of arrangements, and I would just go in and select a few for each session. I did the same thing in Holland with their radio band. But the cutbacks the BBC made in 1970 really hit me hard. There was a recession there, and then my contact in Holland was transferred to another network. I started making exploratory trips back to the States."

Murphy's eventual move back to America after more than ten years was the result of a number of circumstances: Most notably, there was a feeling that a resurgence of jazz was on the horizon. A meeting with an old friend, and a renewed interest in his recording career, convinced Murphy the time was right to return to America.

"I began to notice a new creative force coming over from the States. Cleo Laine did well on a couple of tours and I just smelled that jazz was going to start happening again. It's funny, I was one of the first to settle over here [Europe], anticipating the rock explosion, at a time when nobody would have recorded me in the States anyway, and then I was the first to really sense things were beginning to boil up again in the States. I decided to see for myself.

"I went to see an old friend, Helen Keane, who at the time was managing Bill Evans. We went to a luncheon in New York, and quite by accident, Joe Fields of Muse Records stopped by, and just like that, I was recording again right away. But it took another four or five years for jazz to really pick up though. By that time, I had recorded 'Stolen Moments.' I had written the lyrics years before and just put them away. It just took off like a bird. I even made the charts for a few weeks. I was astounded."

Besides "Stolen Moments," Murphy has also penned lyrics to a number of other jazz instrumentals. Freddie Hubbard's "Red Clay" and Herbie Hancock's "Sly" can be counted among Murphy's contributions. But despite the new wave of success these recordings brought about, Murphy continues to be a regular visitor to Europe, although his home is now in San Francisco. The amount and variety of work is more than enough to keep him coming back to Europe on a regular basis.

"Oh, absolutely," says Murphy. "There's no place in the States I could do a color television show with a sixty-piece orchestra and record with the same setup. The paranoia of advertisers keeps jazz off television in America. You get into these New York offices and they get on that machine gun trip they're into and you're lucky if you get three minutes of their time, and during that three minutes, they're on the phone to somebody else. Those people are on such a speed trip, I can't tell you. Give a guy a telephone and a secretary, and he becomes a different person."

American television and jazz seem to suffer an adversarial relationship, and as Murphy points out, the result is the exposure of a large number of lesser talents at the expense of jazz artists. "Well, they're not stigmatized by the jazz label, in the advertising offices, I mean, not by the performers. Of course I'd rather see Jackie Cain and Roy Kral have their own show. But instead, you have someone like John Davidson, who is a great singer in his own right. But there's still plenty of room for jazz on network television."

Compromise, however, is not part of Murphy's makeup. He has no thoughts about changing his style, even for a lucrative offer. "God, it probably depends on how much money you're talking about. They don't need me, someone already established, to change. They can do that with anybody. Sure it bothers me that I don't have the money that say, Al Jarreau has, but for different reasons. I could probably afford my own trio then, buy some property for my old age. But I say to myself, I'm doing well enough and might even save some money one year. So many good things are happening. I'm pretty content."

Once again an American resident, Murphy has had time to reflect on the different living conditions in Europe and America. Given the choice, he'll opt for San Francisco. "Well, of course London is much more expensive than San Francisco now. Living, I've never had a problem with. Saving money? Yes! I'm not the kind of person who can pinch pennies all the time. I'd rather live well and let the future take its course. But now, I really prefer the States, the life-style as well as the economics. I got tired of certain aspects of living in Europe, certain attitudes. There's so much anti-American feeling in a lot of Europe. France, for example, wants to blame everything on Uncle Sam. I find now that San Francisco has a certain ambiance or mood that I really prefer. The closest thing to it is Holland. You come to Europe and try to fit in with another society and that's when you really find out you're an American and you dig it."

One new aspect of Murphy's career since his return to the States is an involvement with jazz education, and in the process he has given more careful consideration to what jazz means to him. "I've had to think a lot about that lately, since I've gotten into doing clincs. All up and down the West Coast there's a whole new wave of interest in the jazz choir. Dr. Kirby Shaw—he teaches at a small college in northern California—is mainly responsible. I started doing clinics for him and I just found out there's a jazz choir in England at Goldsmith College in Lewisham.

"Anyway, I feel that jazz is a true fusion of cultures—Latin, African, and European. Why it was ever called jazz, I've forgotten. The only thing I can say is that when Count Basie says, 'We're going to play an arrangement by Frank Foster and our trombonist is going to come down front and play a little jazz,' that means it has something to do with the exact art of improvisation. But who knows? In fifty years, we may not call it jazz. Of course, there are always arguments about what jazz is, but really, it doesn't matter what you call it. It's all American music."

Murphy's taste in jazz singers reflects his purist stance, and again underlines the lack of exposure accorded some very large talents. "I've mentioned Jackie and Roy already, and I've only just discovered Sam Fletcher. Andy Bey is another great one, but these people are, unfortunately, singers you just don't hear enough of. I think we're brainwashed with singers. Michael Franks is another good one. He's a prime example of an American singer very much influenced by Brazil, and even though his albums are selling over 200,000 copies, the record company doesn't think it's enough. Like I said, this country is geared on money success.

"The present state of jazz may not be ideal, but I've discovered there is a limited market for noncompromising jazz vocal recordings. My latest record is doing well, and I placed high on the *Downbeat* critic's poll, so I've been able to carve out my little niche. It's not a big one, but it's mine. I'll be able to work in it, probably until I drop dead, and that's probably what I'll have to do."

—London, September 1980

When I first went to
Europe, all I had to do
was tune up to get
applause.
– Eddie 'Lockjaw' Davis

Eddie 'Lockjaw' Davis

"I would never live in Europe," said Eddie "Lockjaw" Davis. "The standard of living is quite different over there. To me, it's like going back twenty-five years in progress. The things we consider necessities in America are luxuries in Europe. If you live in London, for example, you can be on a waiting list for a telephone for up to eighteen months! To me that's primitive. Trying to survive in this business without a telephone is a joke."

A native New Yorker, Davis made his home in Las Vegas until his death in 1986, but he rarely performed there. Instead, he maintained a busy schedule of recording in Los Angeles, and although never a resident of Europe, like so many musicians even today, Davis spent over half of every year there, touring and performing at clubs, concerts, and jazz festivals.

An outspoken, articulate man, Davis was known throughout the jazz world as "Lockjaw" or "Jaws." On one of his first record dates, an enterprising producer in search of a gimmick decided to bill Davis as Dr. Jazz and title all the tunes after medical afflictions. For Davis, "Lockjaw" was the name that stuck.

Davis is perhaps best known for his long association with the Count Basie Band, for which he played the dual role of soloist and road manager. He also led many groups under his own name and enjoyed a prolific recording career, particularly with saxophonist Johnny Griffin. On thirteen albums, they became known as the "tough tenors." It was also Davis who oversaw the historic jam sessions at Minton's Playhouse in New York City during the late fifties.

"It was a policeman's job, and handed to me by Teddy Hill who was the manager at the time. He felt he couldn't manage the club and the bandstand, so he decided whoever was the leader should decide who played and who didn't. How did I qualify to be the judge of who could play and who couldn't? In some instances I was labeled as a tyrant, but on the whole the guys appreciated it. The word spread. If you can't play, don't go on Lockjaw's thing, because he'll ask you off. In doing that, we got the best musicians. It was most relaxed."

In the latter part of 1961 Davis astonished his contemporaries by trading his saxophone for a telephone and becoming a booking agent for Shaw Artists in New York. "At the time," said Davis, "I was running around with some small groups and not going too far. I was beginning to lose interest and when that happens, it's time for a change. It was a good experience and the stepping-stone to becoming road manager for Basie. It also helps me today when I go to Europe. I book my own tours, and as a result I can be selective."

Davis rejoined Basie in 1964, but the combination of administering band business and playing every night eventually wore thin. In 1971 Davis got off the Basie bus for the last time. "It was simply too much to do. First you enjoy the challenge, and then it gets taxing. That's when you learn about Maalox and Bromo-Seltzer."

Davis's world-weary appearance offstage was deceiving. He was easy to talk to and very candid in his observations about jazz in America and Europe. While neither an innovator nor a star in the true sense of the word, Davis was nevertheless always a potent jazz force in the vein of hard-swinging tenor players. And like singer Jon Hendricks, he agreed that America has been reluctant to acknowledge the importance of jazz, an attitude that accounts at least in part for the exodus of American musicians to Europe.

"I think it's for a variety of reasons. It's partly for a better acceptance of your talent as a jazz musician. There's less pressure in terms of competition. Johnny Griffin, for example, lives in a small town in Holland. He doesn't have to fight for a job. He's a big man there, the great American saxophonist. Also the pace of life is slower, so it's definitely a combination of things."

After touring Europe for over twenty-five years, Davis made some sharp comparisons between American and European audiences and the presentation of jazz in general. "When I first went to Europe, all I had to do was tune up to get applause. In America, audiences come out to socialize. Try having music without alcohol. You got a real tired concert. Now in Europe, they don't come out to drink. They're serious listeners. Everyone's got a tape recorder because they want to capture this music, this art. They exchange tapes with friends, talk over the music, but you don't find a lot of drinking. If you have a jazz club in Europe, you can't make it on drinks alone. When the performance is over, you can't find two people to start a card game. They're gone.

"In this country, we stand around, discuss what we've heard, have a drink, get a bite to eat. It's a social thing. In Europe, they want one thing: the music. They have jazz organizations over there that have a different meaning. Record collectors, and other people really into jazz, form groups and have newsletters. They're really involved. That's what makes them more knowledgeable about jazz. It's not simply going to a record store and buying the latest album. They know the history of the artist as well."

Davis learned this firsthand in an incident that vividly illustrates his point. "I was about to join ASCAP, the society of composers. One of the requirements was a list of everything I had ever recorded. Well, I've been recording since the early forties, which would make that quite an undertaking. I was in Copenhagen at the time and a jazz fan heard me talking about this and told me there was a book that showed everything I'd done up to 1972. Try and find something like that in the States. No one is that interested. Records that were made in the twenties would come high in value in Europe. With few exceptions, people here couldn't care less. Those records are up in an attic somewhere."

Davis also agreed that, given the widespread acceptance of jazz in so many countries, its musicians could be used more in some type of ambassadorial role. "Of course, there's no question about it. In South Africa, for example, the State Department sent Dizzy Gillespie, but it was never heralded as a big thing. This was years ago. The idea was to break down the racial thing because it was stipulated in contracts that the audiences were to be mixed. Something like that is a big step, but it's only a token gesture.

"The only thing this country wants to do is break the back of Communism. Any country that's on the verge of turning away from democracy, America jumps up and down and sends all kinds of arms and foreign aid. But to answer your question, certainly there's a lot of room for jazz artists to be utilized to break down barriers, because music, regardless of what kind, *is* universal. There's been a lot of times when jazz has brought peace. In Italy, for example, several jazz groups were sent to where certain factions were not allowed to congregate. But they found a loophole. Give a jazz concert and we can all be in the same hall. The jazz musicians involved quelled near rioting, but you won't read about that. They don't want jazz to have a respectable name."

Despite what Davis saw as token gestures, there is little evidence of any major change in attitude toward jazz. "When they dedicated that park in New Orleans to Louis Armstrong there was a little tid-bit on the news, but certainly no dramatic coverage. Yet this was a man who gave a great deal to this art form. This country thrives on disaster. The hostage situation in Iran, the Cuban refugees coming to Florida—of course they're serious. We'll jump on anything like that, what's supposed to be a humane gesture. We'll donate millions of dollars—Florida was eligible for emergency funds—but do you think you could get that kind of money to subsidize an art form? Never."

In his travels to Europe, Davis came across one opinion expressed by European fans time and again, one he found at first difficult to digest. "European fans, and I've heard this more than once, feel that in the next century, American jazz musicians will be regarded like the painters of past centuries. Maybe there's a point to that."

Constant touring in Europe had its musical hazards. One that Davis shared with other exiles was the former prevalence of unfamiliar, even incompetent, rhythm sections. Davis, however, agreed with many of the exiles that this situation had changed drastically. "Unless it's an all-star group, I play with all Europeans and I defy anyone to tell the difference. Years ago it was a problem. The language barriers meant you could only use your horn to communicate, but now a lot of that has become easier. The musicians know the tunes and are really dedicated. They've come a long way, especially in Scandinavia. England has some fine musicians also but you don't always get them because they're in the studios, which pay more. We have to take the guys that are available, and they're not always the best."

Good musicians or bad, Davis didn't find it a problem working with musicians he was introduced to sometimes only an hour before the performance. "You go with what you have, like a good boxer. You learn to counter. You discover one of the guys is weak, you weave and duck and tip through areas you know you can handle. There's no point in setting a program you know you're going to have trouble with. It's better to just go with standards and blues. The musicians have heard them before and know them, although it does limit your performance."

Davis was in command of a saxophone for more than four decades, and in his own assessment, his playing changed little since his days in the bands of Cootie Williams and Lucky Millinder. "Some things are more relaxed, but basically the style is the same. As long as you're a soloist, the idea in jazz is to develop an identifiable sound. I could take a record I made in 1958 and one I made yesterday and there's really no difference. If you play me a record of Zoot Sims or Ben Webster or Stan Getz—all great tenor players—I can tell the difference because of their tone. If you develop a style, it doesn't vary much over the years. Of course, in recent years we've had some jazz artists going over, going the economic route, getting into rock. But a jazz artist doesn't change much."

"Going over," as Davis called it, was indicative of the newer developments in music—electronics, fusion. He was just as outspoken on these subjects as he was regarding jazz and what the music meant to him. "I think there's room for all kinds of music, although there are some things I've heard that are difficult to call music. But that's just the way our country is. You get a product and if it has mass appeal, it will sell. I don't look at that as an art form. It's simply good promotion. My only point of disagreement is that a lot of the things called jazz should have the word *jazz* left off them. Jazz is an art form and, unfortunately, has few supporters and a minority audience. It will *never* attract a mass audience, not in this country. It's not entertainment. You never see long lines in front of museums, do you?"

It boils down to the familiar Catch-22: Jazz doesn't sell because it isn't promoted; it's not promoted because it doesn't sell. If jazz is rarely heard on television, the situation on radio is not much better. With the exception of certain FM stations and public radio, jazz is seldom heard on the popular airwaves. Increased exposure on radio could certainly enhance the acceptance of jazz in America, but as Davis pointed out, to do so would require a major effort.

"There's no question about it, but again you can't get sponsors. They don't want to school an audience. They want instant ratings. Putting jazz on AM radio would mean educating the masses, and no one wants to go through the initial financial losses to do that. Economics again.

You can have the greatest collection of jazz records, go to a station and donate the records, and still you will not get a sponsor.[1]

"Instead, you get a small FM station with nothing to lose by playing jazz at five o'clock in the morning when everybody is asleep, but that's it. Or, when you do get a guy who gets a break—good station, prime time—right away he changes the program. Instead of playing a decent selection of jazz, he starts playing favorites, sneaks in a little rock, or some disco group his girlfriend likes. First thing you know, he's into a format where everybody says, 'Hey, I thought this was a jazz program.' So even though some people are given the opportunity to do something for jazz, they abuse it. That's too bad because jazz can do a lot of things for a lot of people."

Despite living almost within walking distance of the Las Vegas Hilton, Davis was never tempted by the house band scene that comprises the major employment for musicians in Las Vegas. "No, to me, that's when you lose interest in music and become a politician," Davis said. "You laugh at the conductor's jokes when they're not funny, you lose your identity. It's as simple as that. You cease to create anymore and when you get to that point, you're no longer a jazz musician."

One of his last recordings was with another Las Vegan, singer Joe Williams. The other musicians were so taken with one of Davis's solos that they missed their cue and a second take was required, a rare event on a Davis recording session.

Despite an illness that required major surgery, and eventually led to his death, Davis continued to travel the world jazz circuit where he enjoyed celebrity status. Yet, except through recordings and the interest of serious jazz fans, he remained virtually unknown in his own country. In Las Vegas, he was occasionally spotted in a checkout line at a supermarket, his white Cadillac with the "Jaws" license plate parked outside.

When not relaxing at his Las Vegas home, Davis was content to answer the call for appearances in Europe, the Far East, and the occasional date in New York, Chicago, or Los Angeles, continuing his role as a part-time jazz exile.

—Las Vegas, 1980

Phil Woods

"I just wanted to play jazz," says saxophonist Phil Woods, "and at least I had three jazz gigs in Europe. I didn't have that many in the States, so it couldn't be any worse." [1]

A shortage of jazz gigs is no longer a problem for Phil Woods, and hasn't been for years. Woods now has one of the longest running jazz groups in the business. They work thirty-five weeks per year and changes in personnel have been rare and infrequent. Woods's first date was at age twenty-four, with guitarist Jimmy Raney. But like Dexter Gordon, Johnny Griffin, and a host of others, Woods, despite a background of impressive credentials and credits, had to spend several years in Europe to achieve the acclaim and recognition he enjoys today.

Born and raised in Springfield, Massachusetts, Woods studied briefly with Lennie Tristano, but the bulk of his formal musical education came from the four years he spent at the Julliard School of Music in New York. On-the-job training came with the bands of Dizzy Gillespie, Quincy Jones, and Benny Goodman. Woods's first tour abroad was with the Gillespie band in 1956. He then teamed up with another saxophonist, Gene Quill, for a series of recordings and engagements in the New York area.

In 1959, Woods left for Paris with Quincy Jones in a band that included Melba Liston, Budd Johnson, Joe Harris, Jimmy Cleveland, and future jazz exiles Benny Bailey and Sahib Shihab. The band had been organized for the show *Free and Easy*, and although the show was not a success, many of the musicians remained in Europe when it later folded. Woods returned to New York, but the call for overseas duty came again in 1962, this time for a State Department tour of the Soviet Union with Benny Goodman.

Later, depressed, drinking too much, and having second thoughts about the band he was working with at Birdland, Woods was literally kidnapped by Dizzy Gillespie and Art Blakey, who convinced Woods he should form his own band. "They took me out to Dizzy's house in Long Island," Woods said. "I'd never entertained such a notion. This is a rare profession where people look out for each other that way. It's not a fraternal kind of thing; it's a love thing—taking care of each other.

In 1963, Woods won the *Downbeat* international critics poll in the category of talent deserving wider recognition. But while certainly deserving, the recognition failed to materialize despite his being one of the studio musicians most in demand in New York.

"I was selling cars and Coca-Cola," says Woods. "'Get a flute, then you can double. You'll pick up more jobs.' The flute didn't lead me to music; the alto saxophone led me to music. I don't have any affinity for the flute." The full-time jazz career continued to elude Woods. By 1968, he'd had enough. Accompanied by his wife and three of his five children, Woods left for Europe.

"I was originally headed for Amsterdam, but it was all uncharted territory," says Woods. "I was absolutely flabbergasted at the amount of jazz work I was being offered. After not having worked for a couple of years, I was suddenly headlining at Ronnie Scott's club in London. The European Rhythm Machine [Woods's working band in Europe] was formed instantly with drummer Daniel Humair and two British musicians, bassist Ron Matheson and pianist Gordon Beck. We went right to work playing jazz."

Typically, Woods's success in Europe caused equally immediate results in America, and he received his first invitation to perform at the Newport Jazz Festival. "It's very bizarre. The year after I left the States, I was invited to play at Newport, but not when I lived right around the corner. I guess direct from Paris sounds more exotic than New Hope, Pennsylvania."

Nineteen sixty-eight was a particularly volatile year for America. The Vietnam war was at its peak, the country was reeling from the assassinations of Martin Luther King, Jr., and Robert Kennedy. Student protests and demonstrations were a daily occurrence—all events Woods thought he'd left behind. Paris, however, was no different.

"I was on the corner with my kids buying ice cream when the student riots broke out. Later, coming out of the Metro with my manager, the students were in the street blocking traffic and the Paris police were lined up all across the boulevard. I knew this was trouble but my manager said, 'No problem. The police are very sympathetic to the students' demands.' She was a good manager but she didn't know politics. Our hotel was right in the middle of the battlefield—tear gas, riot police—it was very scary. I was already working at a club in the caves on the Left Bank. Gil Lafite, a good friend and head of the Paris musicians' union, suggested we leave. 'Solidarity with the workers' was the term he used."

When the smoke cleared, Woods and his family moved to an apartment in the Paris suburbs and settled down to the business at hand—playing jazz. The European Rhythm Machine was in constant demand for the next five years. Woods bought a farm thirty miles from Paris and quickly adapted to country life, using France as a base for tours throughout Europe.

"I put the kids in a special school for foreign children to learn French, and they were immediately fluent. They went right into a French school, and even now they've retained their fluency. My son goes back every summer for the wheat harvest and lives like a real Frenchman. Testing your life against another society is good. It did nothing but save my life and made us all better, stronger folks."

Having his own band, Woods managed to avoid a problem that has often plagued the exiles—pickup rhythm sections, where the soloist is introduced to the backing group sometimes only a few hours before the performance. "I did my share of that, but I was lucky. When I worked in Scandinavia, there were already two Americans there, pianist Kenny Drew and drummer Tootie Heath. The bassist was Niels Henning Orsted Pedersen, who is now with Oscar Peterson. So when you're dealing with musicians of that caliber—well, they're right up there with the best players in the world. It's not like it used to be. European musicians have access to the same information we do. The word was that the European rhythm sections couldn't swing, but that's all over now."

Woods's reception and success in Europe point once again to the curious American attitude toward its own music. Equally baffling to Woods is the government's often paradoxical policy toward jazz. "I've worked with three administrations on State Department tours, but there's always been a strange dichotomy between the knowledge at that level—it's good to send jazz all over the world—and the way it's treated in its own country. What America needs is a Voice of America for Americans. With the exception of our own people, we've educated the world about jazz. Yet it seems only suitable for export. The National Endowment for the Arts, I mean it's minuscule, and what the jazz cats get is even smaller, barbaric. But in Europe, with subsidization and nationalized radio, by dictate, jazz gets a hefty percentage. Now I don't know if it's a suitable solution for us, but all over the world jazz is revered. Here, it's barely tolerated."

Woods agrees, however, that it's not only jazz that is well received in Europe. "They're more aware of the arts in general. You can see that in the buildings, statues, museums, and in their regard for literature. And since jazz is the most vibrant creation, perhaps in the twentieth century—I believe it was Kurt Vonnegut who said, 'historians will thank us for our sense of humor and our music'—they really get into listening to jazz."

European audiences listened to Woods for five years, but by 1972 he began to pay for his success. As with Don Byas before him, the work tapered off, and he was told to scale things down, lower his fee, and stop his illusions of grandeur.

"It was a very strange rationale and I couldn't accept it. Some of it is the mystique that Europeans understand American music better than Americans. I'm not so sure about that. They like to play the role—at least in France—of 'America doesn't understand you. Come over here and we'll give you a gig because *we* do.' That only works if you're unknown. Once you get a reputation and you're recognized in the States, then you're nothing in Europe. It's very snobbish, I think. They also really have a thing against white musicians. I know that for a fact. Is Morris Lane a bigger contributor to jazz than Bill Evans? That's as ridiculous as the critics who say white players can't swing like blacks. I've seen them [critics] at concerts snapping their fingers on the wrong beat. Don't tell me they know swinging more than anybody else. Watch them snap their fingers. They have no rhythm at all and that goes for critics all over, not just in Europe. The whole thing in Europe is, there are two camps: Hugues Panassie and Charles Delaunay. Panassie supposedly hated bebop and Delaunay is the champion of modern jazz. The only reason for that split is they were both sent bebop records [to review] but Panassie's were lost in the mail. It's an institution in France, but it was purely an accident. Ridiculous!"

Despite his later experiences and reservations about Europe, Woods is nevertheless emphatic that without an extended European stay, his current success wouldn't have happened. "No it wouldn't. If I hadn't gone to Europe when I did, I would have probably bought that flute and ended up in Los Angeles playing on the Johnny Carson or Merv Griffin show, or something like that, sticking the profits up my nose or in my arm and been very unhappy. That's the only future I could foresee at the time. I'll be forever grateful to the European audiences for giving me the artistic confidence, listening, and saying, 'Yeah, you can play.' Without that, I couldn't have come back and continued. Those were very good years for the music."

Europe, however, is not an experience Woods recommends for everyone. "I get a lot of young musicians who say, 'Man, you went to Europe and you spent five years there and it really seemed to solidify your career. Should I do that?' I always recommend against it. First you've got to make your mark here . . . then it's easy because then Europe says, 'Ah, he did okay in America. He must be able to play.' This is still, to them, the final arbiter of who can play and who can't play. They don't know."

Still there is no question about the experience being a positive one for Woods. "Personally, the move was great for my family. We had the Paris *Herald-Tribune*, that great French food and wine, so I found it hard to miss anything. I did miss the camaraderie of the American jazz musician. The European players didn't have that, as well as they played. I never really felt at home in Europe. I found France a bit too formal. Nobody invites you to their home until you've known them for years. I mean I'm an American, man. I understand this country and I love it. But for perspective, there's nothing like getting away and checking it out."

Despite the critical success of the European Rhythm Machine, which included a Grammy nomination for *Live in Frankfurt*, Woods began to be treated as a local by the very people who had lauded his arrival five years earlier.

"If it was going to be like that, I figured I might just as well go home. Dexter Gordon was going back periodically, Johnny Griffin, Sahib Shihab, and Art Farmer were making trips back; the chickens were coming home to roost. Jean-Luc Ponty, Dave Pike, and I all had bands, the only three established groups in Europe. It was a strange coincidence that we all split at the same time and ended up in Los Angeles within ten days of each other."

Woods's homecoming was not a triumphant one, at least not at first. His first year back, he worked a total of three nights. Ironically, he was rescued by a Frenchman. "Who would have thought that my artistic salvation would be at the hands of Michel Legrand, who, it turns out, lived in the next town from where my farm was in France. But in the five years I lived there, I never once saw Michel."

Woods's newfound association with Legrand led to a recording contract with RCA Victor and the formation of Woods's current group, which includes drummer Bill Goodwin and bassist Steve Gilmore as charter members. Pianist Hal Galper replaced Mike Mellelo in 1980. That was the first personnel change in seven years. More recently, Woods added trumpeter Tom Harrell.

Woods returned to Pennsylvania and now makes his home in the Pocono Mountains when he isn't touring the world. Wedged among the rounds of clubs, concerts, and festivals in Australia, Europe, Africa, and South America, Woods manages to continue working with young people in clinics. He began the practice years ago when he directed the jazz department at Rambleny, a summer arts camp in New Hope, Pennsylvania.

"It's missionary work and makes for future audiences. I love talking to kids. They're the best audience we have. Ninety percent of our fans are young people, not the old standbys from the Birdland days."

Woods has definite ideas about the curriculum he would use if he were to teach at a college. "I would charter a bus and get all the kids and I'd have them get their libraries together and their music stands. I'd get uniforms for them. Have them get all their crap together, pack it and get on the bus, close all the blinds, and just drive around the campus for about eight hours—don't go anywhere, no visual delights to intrigue them, just whatever they want to do. Get off the bus, set up, pick out a set, tune up, put their uniforms on. That's it; they're not going to play any music. Pack up, back on the bus another eight hours, circle some more, then have a talk with them: 'All right, now, who wants to do this? Because this is what it is.' It's an exaggeration. I admit it doesn't have to be that way, but it's just an exaggerated reality, because they're not getting any reality in school. Most of the teachers have never been on the road. They're the cats that couldn't make it, so they went back to teach it. Some of them are qualified, dedicated men—don't get me wrong; I'm not rapping them. I'm just saying the colleges, the powers that be, have got to take advantage of people like me and all the pros—have us visit them and tell them."

Pros like Ben Webster are who Woods has in mind. "Why don't we have a jazzman-in-residence in universities? Why did Ben Webster have to die in Europe alone? Why wasn't he given a post? Jazzman-in-residence—give him all the beer he wants and a room. 'Ben, you don't have to do nothing. Just stop by the jazz department if you feel like rapping with the kids.' Now you know human nature and so do I. You'd make that man so proud he'd probably cool his drinking. He'd live longer. He'd contribute to the kids. We don't think of those things. They're afraid to take a chance: 'Maybe Ben would go ape.' Well, we've had poets go ape on campus before; it's very chic for a poet to go ape on campus."[2]

And what of those other young people, that profusion of rock stars who have crowded jazz in recent years. "I don't care," says Woods. "It's pop art. It's got nothing to do with what I do. We're not supposed to be popular musicians. There's a very fine line between art and entertainment. What was Louis Armstrong? He was the greatest entertainer and a great artist as well, but that's more toward the show business side than I want to do. There's enough of an audience for the band now that I can just go for the art thing and honestly present the music. So if three kids make a million dollars a night with three chords—great. It's nothing to do with making my task easier or harder.

"It does bother me when a jazz musician does it and they call it jazz. You find the more money a jazz musician makes, the less his contribution to jazz seems to be. I mean George Benson was a great jazz guitarist, but now that he's got some money, he's not so great? No way! He's still a great jazz player. We are so confused by all this nonsense that it's hard to keep your head on straight. I just try not to let it interfere with what I'm doing. I know my market. I'm at the top of my profession. The audience I have is devoted and understands what I'm doing—maybe a bit noisy, but that's a saloon attitude. They're noisy in Europe too. This propaganda about Europe understanding culture more than we do—well, maybe they are a little older, but they are not necessarily better. Perhaps some of the rudest audiences I've seen have been in Paris, Berlin, Bologna. That always intrigues me: Europe has never produced one jazz musician. I'm leaving out Stephane Grappelli and Django Reinhardt; they are exceptions. I'm talking about out of all the players, not many major figures. More is not necessarily better. More just means you get some ignorant people who don't know what you're doing."

Not enough people in America do know what jazz musicians are doing, a fact Woods regrets; but perhaps more important, he believes in a direct connection between jazz and America that goes beyond the music.

"It's bad enough when they ignore your music, but when they put down your life-style, and yet really need that life-style that we've all been through with cats on the road, well, that's just too much. To the average American, jazz musicians are wastrels, terrible people. And yet, we get along on very little. We improvise. We're not at a total loss when something goes wrong. We can all cook a little, fix a car a little. We're all sort of renaissance men in our own small way. That whole sharing thing, recycling old ideas, old band uniforms—old ladies. Talk about conserving natural resources! You ain't got it, you make do with what you got, and if there's ever a time for that, it's right now. We've lost that as Americans. There's a great philosophical lesson here that's being totally ignored. The whole idea of American jazz is that it's built on improvisation, as is this country. Maybe someday America will look to jazz for just that concept."

Although he still maintains his farm in France, Woods's future plans call for no extended return to Europe. "No, but I can always spend some time eating and drinking in the south of France. Touring once a year is enough. I'd kind of like to make it in Japan for a couple of years, and there's other places I'd like to explore.[3] It's only logical. Nothing is forever. You gotta keep moving."

—Chicago, 1981

12

Jon Hendricks

"I went on a tour across country the summer of the riots—Cleveland, Detroit—and got back home just in time for the one in San Francisco. Plus, there was so much dope in the schools around there, hell, everywhere. We decided to get our kids out of there. Europe seemed like the logical place, so I called Ronnie Scott in London and got a gig there for a month. That was extended for another month, and that was the start of the whole thing."

During his second month at Ronnie Scott's, Hendricks was voted the number-one jazz singer by *Melody Maker*, edging out Louis Armstrong and Ray Charles. "That put me almost in the category of pop artist," says Hendricks. "I started getting calls from the BBC and all over Europe so I just decided to stick around and ride it out. The next year, it was the same thing."

Artistically and personally, Jon Hendricks's five-year stay in Europe, begun in 1968, proved to be a period of rediscovery. European audiences, many of them holdovers from the Lambert, Hendricks & Ross era, were joined by a host of new, younger fans, who discovered Jon Hendricks the soloist. The experience bolstered the singer's own beliefs regarding the struggles of jazz artists, particularly black ones.

"If a person likes jazz in America, all his neighbors come down on him. Now, that's a helluva pressure. You know how many cats start playin' jazz and their parents want them out of the house? I'm not talking about spooks. I mean young white kids who take up jazz. Their parents react as if they've joined some religious cult or something. In Europe, these conditions just don't apply. There's a straight line from the artist to the audience that doesn't exist in America, and the real underlying reason can be traced directly to slavery."

Singer, educator, composer, writer—Jon Hendricks can lay claim to all and continues to mold what has become one of the most multifaceted careers in jazz. As one of the music's most articulate spokesmen, Hendricks is also its most relentless crusader. He began his career as a drummer, but once he heard Roy Haynes, he pawned his drums and has been a singer ever since. Haynes, however, was the first drummer to work with Lambert, Hendricks & Ross.

Born in Toledo, Ohio, Hendricks was working in local clubs by age thirteen in such fast company as Art Tatum and Charlie Parker. Encouraged by these and other musicians, especially Parker, Hendricks forsook his plans for a law career and eventually moved to New York. His early days were spent in an office typing invoices. By night, he haunted the jazz clubs and labored over lyrics, often written to recorded instrumental solos that laid the groundwork for an idea still in its embryo stage.

The group's big break came with the recording of *Sing a Song of Basie* in 1957. Hendricks and Dave Lambert had already recorded "Four Brothers" and "Cloudburst." Annie Ross joined the two men and a new group was born. By 1958, while the scientific world reeled from the Russian launching of Sputnik I, the jazz world was turned upside down by the vocal antics of a trio whose name sounded more like a law firm than a jazz group. Lambert, Hendricks & Ross launched into their own orbit and were quickly touted as the hottest vocal group in jazz.

"I called us The Metropolitan Bopera," says Hendricks. The trio enjoyed tremendous popularity for several years before Annie Ross became ill during an engagement in Frankfurt, Germany, and returned to her native England. Yolanda Bavan replaced Ross in 1962, but for Hendricks, it was never the same without Ross. "Annie was unique," Hendricks said. Hendricks returned to solo performing and Dave Lambert went back to the New York studios until he was tragically struck down while changing a tire one rainy night near Westport, Connecticut.

The group's influence, however, has spread even beyond jazz into the world of pop music. Lyricist Hendricks, once dubbed the James Joyce of jazz for his creation and vocalese performance of instrumental solos, has to date had a hand in over three hundred compositions. In 1979, his collaboration with pianist Joe Zawinul netted Manhattan Transfer a Grammy for "Birdland," and opened new doors for Hendricks.

"Birdland" was orginally written for another vocal group, The Swingle Singers, but when they didn't have time to add it to their session, it went to Manhattan Transfer. "They told me they had a couple of tracks open, so I said, I got a song for you."

But Jon Hendricks and a pop group, even one as musical as Transfer, seems at first glance a strange alliance. Hendricks's view of the popular music scene, however, is something of a departure for a jazz musician.

"I also deplore the low state of the music, with certain exceptions, but I see further. Even that has something good about it because I remember when "ofays"[1] couldn't clap their hands on two and four. But thanks to rock, sociologically at least, the way has been paved for the mass acceptance of jazz for the first time in the history of America. And that's an important step."

Peering at the world through thick glasses, the diminutive Hendricks is ever aware of his role as a jazz artist in an almost spiritual way. He often refers to himself as a student and scholar. His speech, while sprinkled with street jargon, is a blend of philosophical musings and social commentary gleaned from years of firsthand experience both at home and abroad with the struggles of the jazz artist.

"In America, we're still viewed as ex-slaves, however liberal the thinking. The main reason jazz is not as popular in America is because when you start playing jazz, you forget all about that shit. But the powers that be are thinking just the opposite. They're thinking in terms of racism all the time. They don't want no music that brings people together without thought or differences. That's why jazz has such a hard time in this country. The Europeans never had us as slaves, so they can accept it for what it is—groovy music. Americans could like it the same way but the social system makes it impossible."

Hendricks's comments reflect in part the treatment he received in the U.S. Army. Racial hostilities between black and white soldiers prompted Hendricks and four friends to go AWOL. The quintet ended up in Dijon, France, where they survived for a year. When the Army caught up with them and threatened hanging, Hendricks explained the circumstances of their absence and the penalty was reduced to three years at the U.S. Army detention center in Marseilles. Hendricks served eleven months.

The attitude of American youth is most encouraging to Hendricks, for the music as well as for racial issues. "The young kids are not making the same mistakes because they don't have the same motivation as their elders to maintain those old standards—economics.

It's all based on money. There's no hatred involved, don't nobody hate nobody, especially whites and spooks. If you got a cook, it's a spook in the kitchen. If you got somebody taking care of your kids, it's one of us. How you gonna hate someone when you got them cooking your meals and taking care of your kids? Anytime you see a group of kids together, you see spooks, Chinese, whites, whatever. They're not worried about that stuff and that's the greatest friend jazz ever had. No, it all boils down to money. But the kids are changing all that. All that old stuff is fading. It looks like it's never moving but you look at five years ago and then look now. It's slowly shucking off because as these old people die, that's the end of it. As for the future of jazz, it's wonderful, especially since we face an economic crisis. When has jazz been most popular? In the midst of severe economic times. What did they call the jazz age? The depression. Every time this country falls on hard times, jazz goes up. Things look good for us."

Hendricks continues to be optimistic and senses a change of attitude on the horizon. "More and more Americans are traveling to Europe and finding out the only thing any other country wants from us besides money is jazz. Hell, everything else is theirs already. Europeans don't want to know about ballet, that's Russian. Painting is French, Shakespeare is English. The only thing they want to know about from us is Louis Armstrong and Duke Ellington—jazz. And as someone once said—maybe it was me—if you don't know nothin' about that, you just a damn fool! Our government has got to stop spending money on opera. That ain't got nothing to do with us. Jazz is our contribution. You know where Reagan was at when he cut the arts programs and spent all the money on defense instead."

A staunch supporter of Jimmy Carter for his interest in jazz—"He sang 'Salt Peanuts' with me and Dizzy at the White House"—Hendricks saw the Reagan administration as a last-ditch stand of a dying order. "They're all dead, they just haven't fallen over yet. The kids are not taking up that old zeal. Even Senator [Charles] Percy, a Republican, had to come out and say Reagan's nominee for human rights spokesman was not fit for the job because there are too many spooks voting now."

With a future in Europe assured, Hendricks transferred his ASCAP royalties to satisfy British immigration and settled in London in 1968. He enrolled his children in a private school specializing in music and art. His rented home near Hyde Park became something of an overseas club for visiting musicians and performers, sporting as well a fair sampling of British nobility. In addition to numerous appearances at Ronnie Scott's club, Hendricks played all over Europe at clubs and festivals, made a number of appearances on British and European television,[2] and recorded for the Phillips label in England.

One of his most memorable engagements was a two-month stay at a small club in Stockholm that was inaugurating a jazz policy. But traveling there had rather humorous consequences. Leaving from London, a curious three-car caravan (with Hendricks, his wife Judith, four children, a nanny, and a rhythm section consisting of Reg Powell, Darryl Runswick, Bill Moody, and Rebop Kwakubah) crossed the Swedish frontier with Hendricks himself at the wheel of the lead vehicle, a massive, black Austin Princess. To the amazement of Hendricks's troop, hordes of people turned out to watch the motorcade pass through towns and villages en route to Stockholm.

"I found out later, the only car like that in Sweden belonged to the king," laughs Hendricks. Stockholm resident Red Mitchell replaced Runswick on bass, and by closing night Hendricks had a legion of new fans who presented the singer and his band with large bouquets of flowers. But the audience was typical Hendricks fare. "Every time I got up on the stand everybody got happy because they knew what I was going to do—the only trick I know: swing like a dog!"

Back in England, Hendricks continued to work regularly at jazz pubs and Ronnie Scott's. On several of those engagements, he was reunited with Annie Ross, now fully recovered and pursuing an acting career.[3] Returning home in the early seventies to celebrate the birth of his sister-in-law's new baby, Hendricks received an offer that prompted him to stay in the United States. The position of jazz critic for the *San Francisco Chronicle* was suddenly vacant due to the death of Ralph Gleason. Anxious to spend some time away from the rigors of the road, and intrigued by the offer, Hendricks responded to this new challenge with characteristic eagerness. His knowledgeable commentary was often biting and, for once, jazz was being written about by a musician. Hendricks says the *Chronicle*'s editor called him "the only honest columnist I've ever had."

It was during this same period that Hendricks was able to realize a long-held ambition to teach. He was approached by the University of California, Berkeley, to take over the reins of a jazz history course. Jazz in American Society was an immediate and resounding success. "Six hundred and fifty students signed up for the class," Hendricks says proudly. "They were out in the hallway, on the steps, even hanging around outside. We finally had to move the class to an auditorium but still had to turn away about another hundred students. That really showed me how much kids want to know about jazz. And the questions they asked sent *me* to the books for some of them."

Like the other jazz exiles, Hendricks counts his stay in Europe an artistic and rewarding experience. Given the opportunity, he wouldn't hesitate to go again. "I like the style of living, the atmosphere, culturally and artistically. It's just a better climate for the artist. I mean why should there be other pressures than the one of just pursuing your art? This idea of an artist trying to make a living is ridiculous. When you have to spend the best hours of the day just trying to pay the rent, it robs the world of art. What we've got to do is adopt the best facets of socialism just as they've got to adopt the best things about the capitalist system. This country is so busy making money that people don't realize that after making all that money, you've got to be able to enjoy it. Certainly it would help if you have some sense of art and culture, particularly your own.

"But going to Europe was a blessing in disguise for me. I learned more about the political scene in America while living in Europe, because of one thing. I had access to news programs that were never shown in America. Hell, a lot of Americans thought all Cubans looked like Desi Arnaz. But also, I came to understand that it is possible for an artist to live a good, quiet life. You don't have to eat on the run, you can take three hours for lunch if you feel like it. This fast food in America, the money you save eventually goes to a doctor. The European style of life taught me that you should put more time into just living. Just being alive and enjoying life. In this country, everything is going so fast, nobody just sits down and says what a nice day it is. The pace is so fast and you don't even know what you're moving toward."

Hendricks's greatest single contribution to jazz is perhaps his show, *Evolution of the Blues*, a tour de force of blues and jazz singing that spans the spectrum of the music from slave chants to the bebop licks of Charlie Parker. Joe Williams, Jimmy Witherspoon, and Jimmy Rushing also joined Hendricks in a number of the show's performances. Commissioned by Jimmy Lyons, director of the Monterey Jazz Festival, Hendricks describes *Evolution* as "the story of every Negro person in America." The show was a huge success at Monterey, and later Hendricks performed it at the Newport Jazz Festival and Carnegie Hall. It was reborn following Hendricks's return from Europe. A blend of music, history, poetry, and social commentary, *Evolution* enjoyed a five-year run in San Francisco before moving to a small theater in the shadow of the UCLA campus in Westwood, California.

"We were there for over a year although nothing previously had run for more than six weeks. We'd still be there if the producers hadn't stolen the show." Hendricks was engaged in a lengthy legal battle to regain rights and with the success of *Ain't Misbehavin'* and *Sophisticated Ladies*, he hoped one day to take the show to Broadway. Hendricks believes *Evolution of the Blues* was the inspiration for every type of jazz-based show since.

But can the inherent quality of jazz be maintained with anything like a mass audience? Hendricks thinks so. "When you spread anything to a mass audience you always lower the standards. If you have a French restaurant that serves thirty people and then expands to serve three hundred, the food has got to drop in quality, unless you stick to your guns. That's what jazz artists have got to do. Now I think the jazz artists who have found intellectual reasons for going into the rock thing—reasons like fusion and all that other shit—is really just a case of, man, I want to make me some money. Look what happens to them. Cats like Chick Corea are now trying to swing again. I had a nineteen-year-old pianist from Japan playing like Oscar Peterson. He ain't been messin' with no fusion. European musicians, even Japanese, are keeping our culture alive by playing jazz."

Hendricks is an equally acerbic critic of the media, citing their failure to showcase jazz despite the opportunities he feels are present. "On the 'Tonight Show,' for example, they have this wonderful band but they can't play anything except during commercials. But you notice when they come back, the studio audience is yelling and screaming for the band." He also never misses an opportunity to lecture record company executives on their failure to give jazz its rightful due. "The record companies also have a responsibility, a cultural responsibility to make sure jazz is recorded, to serve society. But what happens is that many record companies are owned by larger conglomerates that also own night clubs, and naturally, they push the artists they have under contract in those clubs."

Hendricks had yet another run-in with record companies when he decided to attempt a version of the Miles Davis classic, "Freddy Freeloader," one of the many jazz standards for which Hendricks has penned lyrics. No American company would offer more than $25,000 for the album, despite Hendricks's choice of commercially viable singers Bobby McFerrin, George Benson, and Al Jarreau to join him.[4] Denon Records of Japan came to the rescue, financed the entire session, and in 1990 the *Freddy Freeloader* album was a Grammy nominee. Hendricks just smiles. "Nothing much has changed."

Today, Jon Hendricks is back on the road, spreading the gospel of jazz with a new group, and this time sharing the vocal duties with wife Judith and often his son Eric. He carries his own rhythm section despite admitting, "I don't really make the money that entitles me to, but it's so much better having your own group backing you."

Hendricks agrees with Phil Woods that American artists often have to go to Europe to make it, and he has no doubts about jazz being America's music. "The music of America *is* jazz," Hendricks says emphatically. "They've tried all this other stuff—country and western, rock—but it's all got to come back to jazz. Ain't no place else to go. Where else can you find beauty, honesty, and artistry except in jazz?"

—London, Stockholm, Chicago, 1969, 1981

13

*I feel at home in Pittsburgh
or Kansas City but when I go
to Paris I feel wet-eyed.
– Nathan Davis*

Nathan Davis

When Nathan Davis first saw *'Round Midnight,* a film based on the sixties' Paris jazz scene, he wasn't sure he could stay through the whole picture. "It was too close to home for me, and pretty accurate," Davis says from his office at the University of Pittsburgh, where since 1969 he's been the director of the Jazz Studies program.

Davis has done several interviews about the film. His only regret is that the producers didn't use the Paris Reunion Band for the sound track. "It's almost like a documentary," Davis says, recalling the film. "That could have been like my life except for the strung-out part. It was one of the best periods of jazz."

The Paris Reunion Band was founded by Davis and other musicians from the American jazz colony in the fifties and sixties. Their goal was to recreate the Paris atmosphere musically, and to pay tribute to drummer Kenny Clarke, Davis's mentor and longtime friend. Davis was already in Europe when he met Clarke, Benny Bailey, and Joe Harris. Following his discharge from the Army in 1960, Davis elected to remain in Europe.

"I had decided," Davis says. "You could stay one year and still get a free trip back courtesy of the Army, but by then I was working with all these great musicians so I said the hell with it. Jacquin Berendt put together an expatriate concert and Kenny Clarke invited me to go to Paris and join his band."

Living in Berlin for six months, Davis married a German girl and quickly installed himself in Paris. "I was there [Paris] except for the last six months before I came back," Davis says. "I took an apartment in Brussels then." His first house guest was fellow exile bassist Red Mitchell, who was then on his way to Stockholm.

It was Kenny Clarke again who encouraged Davis to return to the United States in 1969 and take up his present position at the University of Pittsburgh. Davis calls Clarke "the Dean, my father; we were very close. When he said go, I went. I ran a jazz program every summer in Paris for Richard Roy, who had originally started the program. David Baker [University of Indiana] recommended me to Pittsburgh and called me in Paris. Klook said, 'Go and tell the truth.' At first I wasn't going, but when I talked to Klook, he said, 'Go, do it, we need people like you in those positions.' I invited him over several times and once he took over for me for a semester. Klook never wanted to come back."

Since his return to the States, Davis, who holds a Ph.D. in ethno-musicology from Wesleyan University, in Connecticut, has maintained a balance between performing jazz and immersing himself in the academic life. For the most part, there are no regrets.

"What happened to Dex [Gordon] and [Phil] Woods didn't happen to me because I went into academia. I didn't go on tour, leave my job. I made up my mind to teach and be here. Consequently I probably lost out on some things, but I don't regret the move. I still tour."

Born in Kansas City, Kansas, in 1937, Davis grew up in a musical family. By age eighteen, he was working with Jay McShann. He won a scholarship to the University of Kansas where he earned a B.A. in Music Education, and led a band that included trumpeter Carmel Jones.

The Nathan Davis perspective on the exile life offers an inside look into the Paris jazz scene in the sixties as well as an educator's view on where jazz has gone since. During his ten-year stay in Europe, Davis returned to America only once for an Army music competition in 1961. If anything, Davis says he became more American as a result of his foreign residence.

"I consider myself a citizen of the world who happened to find work in France," Davis says. "I wasn't anti-American or anything like that. I was glad I had a gig, playing with Dizzy, Sonny Criss, Dex [Gordon], Klook [Kenny Clarke]—all were sitting in when, here I was, just out of the Army and trying to get it together. Where was I supposed to go? I was and still am somebody who believes in a united utopia—no borders, no passports, no currency differences. I'm kind of like that. I knew I was American, but I had never really intended to come back."

There were occasions, however, when Davis felt the pull of his roots, feelings that were triggered by music. "A few times, when I worked with Ray Charles and he started singing "Georgia," I started crying. Also when I heard black gospel music, I'd get homesick. I did a television show, playing the role of Sidney Bechet. The whole idea was everybody would gather in Paris with the Reverend Sergeant of the

American church. It was like Harlem in Paris. There would be certain occasions, but I knew I wasn't French. You know, I'm not sure what would have happened if I had stayed."

Had he stayed in Paris, and Davis has often thought about it, his life might have been quite different. "There's a couple of ways of looking at it. I did my first recordings over there. One of my records recently sold for 200 pounds in London. It's a collector's item. *Happy Girl*, my first record, was written up in magazines all over Europe. If I had made that same record in America, with publicity and money—well, who knows? Europeans called it art. Now I have a hit. A record I made in 1978 is a hit now. Things happen. There's a certain exotic look to cats who stayed over there."

By the sixties, one of the most popular places in Paris was the Mars Club on the city's Right Bank. Bob Dorough had spent time there and, like Dorough, Davis remembers it not only for the music, but as something of a celebrity hangout. There were two other American pianists in residence, Art Simmons and Aaron Bridges. "It was like a piano bar," Davis says of the Mars Club. "What was important about it was wherever they went [Simmons and Bridges], that was where the people went. Sidney Poitier, Martin Luther King, Elizabeth Taylor, musicians, writers, actors—everyone went there."

With the proliferation of American musicians in Paris during this period, Davis too experienced a certain resentment from the French jazz community. "Yeah, I remember one time I came off the bandstand just before it started. This one saxophone player came up to me, blocked my path, and said, 'You're taking work because you're black.' All that kind of stuff. It was really embarrassing because the club was crowded and Saturday night. I told him he could go and work in America if he wanted and mentioned some French musicians who had done so. 'Jean-Luc Ponty, Martial Solal, Michel Legrand, these cats work, so just go.' I'm here," Davis told the Frenchman, "because I like living here.

"We were not permitted to do everything," Davis says, "but we used to make a lot of movies, do studio work. We could be soloists or composers so it worked out better. We got star money and that worked better for us. That was the agreement we had with the French musicians' union."

The union, however, continued to feel pressure from French musicians and were forced to attempt a policy that would limit the number of American musicians working in Paris. "We were kind of taking over," Davis says. "That, coupled with the times, caused them to form a syndicate and announce a boycott of the clubs. The owners were not to hire American musicians except for established cats like Klook. It didn't last long. Madame Ricard, who owned a club, stood up and defied them, said she would close her club, as did Ben Benjamin, who ran the Blue Note. I got letters from people all over Europe to come and live with them and work."

While the music opportunities may have been better in Paris, the business side of things was all too familiar to Davis and other American musicians living and touring in France. "Those promoters can be vicious," Davis says. "I remember a scene at the Antibes Jazz Festival. Louis [Armstrong] came over and they wanted Klook to play with him for a lot less money. Klook said, 'I love Pops, but they give him all the money. I'm not going to do it.' I made good enough money to make a living though," says Davis.

Returning from his honeymoon with his German wife, Ursula, Davis found the scene in Paris changed during his brief absence. "We got married in Berlin and had a holiday there. When we came back, the club was sold and it was a disco. Just like that I was out of a gig. When we were playing there, there were lines outside the club even on a Tuesday night."

Although working often with Kenny Clarke and touring with Art Blakey and the Jazz Messengers, Davis sometimes found himself in front of a European rhythm section. "Sometimes it was a problem. When I first went over there I used to hear them [musicians] talk about that. I worked with Dolphy and my own groups but most of the time I worked with Klook. But Joe Ney and Alex Riel [drummers] were two non-Americans everyone liked to work with. Peter Trunk, a bassist, was also excellent. He was a student of O.P. [Oscar Pettiford]. He could walk his ass off. But when you got past those cats it got a little funny sometimes. Pony Poindexter said (Charles Lloyd was coming over with Keith [Jarrett], Ron [McClure], and Jack [DeJonette]) Charles can't strike out with that rhythm section. Now, that's no longer the case. You can find a good one anywhere. They got it together now. They've been more exposed to American rhythm sections. They could learn the lines, but they still had to play with you to get the feel, the shit would kind of seep in. That's something to experience. Once at the Blue Note with Donald Byrd and Art Taylor, Woody Shaw came to me and said, 'I sound like I'm playing a toy trumpet.' By then, Davis himself was assuming a kind of mentor role for younger musicians. Shaw was among them. "I brought Woody over for three or four years. When Horace Silver offered him a gig, he asked me what to do. I said it's a good shot for you. Go."

With the music scene being what it was, with many American musicians in Paris, Davis missed little about America. "Well, not really. A lot of guys that drink, they did. Booze was available from the American Embassy PX if you wanted it. Ben Benjamin had cats bringing him liquor. I was smoking at the time but I didn't like French cigarettes. But mainly it was gospel and blues music that I missed. Memphis Slim was living there at the time. It reminded me of family. I missed football a little bit but I got into soccer. I missed some foods. Johnny Griffin and I used to have chili contests and invite all the cats over."

Audiences too were different but not necessarily better than American ones. "In a way, American audiences, there's a lot made about the difference and in a way it's true, but I don't want to bang American audiences. What you find in America is you have a lot of fringe jazz lovers. There are more purists in Europe, they're more knowledgeable, that's the part that's different. That's also true in America but there are probably not as many. Here in Pittsburgh, for example, there's a great jazz audience. They don't go for the publicity thing, the hype, they're more pure jazz oriented. What's really crazy," says Davis, "is Tokyo. I stepped off a bus there and a guy just started running down my whole history, and I'm not Miles."

By 1968, the complexion of the Paris scene was changing considerably. The student riots brought about a different atmosphere in the City of Light. "With the revolution, shit started to fall apart," Davis says. "There was tear gas in the clubs, not as much work. The St. Germain and other clubs closed. Some new places popped up in the seventies but there was a dry spell where there wasn't much happening. Some guys were leaving Paris, moving on. I took Griff's [Johnny Griffin's] and my wife out of the country to Belgium, then to Holland."

Despite his academic responsibilities, Davis still finds time to tour either with his own group Tomorrow, or the Paris Reunion Band, which is scheduled for another major tour. Davis also periodically returns to Europe for guest appearances with a number of European radio bands.

Today, Davis sees the American jazz scene much improved, and exposure to the public with films like 'Round Midnight and Clint Eastwood's film Bird have, Davis feels, contributed a great deal to this improvement. "It [Bird] was more accurate than the Billie Holiday story.[1] It's good to expose more people to Charlie Parker," Davis says. His own doctoral dissertation was written on Parker. "There was some controversy about black musicians not being contacted with film people. Walter Bishop, Jr., for example, was never called and he was Bird's pianist. Dizzy wasn't hired but they might have talked to him. Overall though it was a very positive film. You've got to make it work dramatically, and the music was great the way they did that using Bird and a modern rhythm section. Still it's never perfect. There's a biography on my life out now by a German writer and I've already got a few people mad at me. You leave somebody out, don't mention something. Both films, though, were very positive contributions to the literature of jazz."

Today, Davis continues to make his home in Pittsburgh. Having lived there for many years, he feels at home there and in his native Kansas City. Still, the pull of Paris is a strong one. "When I go to Paris I feel wet eyed. My daughter was born there. The most productive part of jazz in Paris was when I was there, it was my prime. I traveled so much then, when I'd land at Orly Airport, I felt I was getting ready to get home. It was like home, so now when I go to Paris and stay in a hotel, it feels strange."

Davis's last engagement before returning to America was at the Golden Circle club in Stockholm. It was the end of an era for Davis but one he continues to carry with him. "The greatest thing, other than the music, was that it really broadened my concept of life and gave me a certain confidence, a totally awakening experience educationally. I had never studied a foreign language, and then there was the racial difference. I ran into little or no prejudice there. It's hard to separate it from the music. We were looked at as special. I would advise anybody to go and live in a foreign culture, especially in one so rich as France."

—Pittsburgh, 1991

14

No matter how long you live in
a country, you wind up realizing
you're an American jazz musician
living in Sweden.
— Red Mitchell

Red Mitchell

With the exception of 1951, bassist Keith "Red" Mitchell has been playing jazz on a regular basis since 1948. He began the jazz life at the Onyx Club on 52nd Street opposite Charlie Parker's quintet. By then, Mitchell had been listening to jazz for years, learning clarinet, alto saxophone, and piano by ear.

Mitchell's first instrument was the piano—one he still plays—but he discovered the bass in 1947 while working with a U.S. Army band in Europe. "They sent me to Germany, and I just lucked out," Mitchell says. "I got into a big band that only played jazz. Every Sunday night we did a show called 'It's Only Yours.' We slept all day and jammed all night."

Mitchell paid for his first bass with twelve cartons of cigarettes. In 1992, as he contemplates a return to America after twenty-four years in Europe, Mitchell has five basses. Two occupy space in a Stockholm apartment with Mitchell and his sociologist wife, Diane; one is in New York; another is in Los Angeles; and still another resides in Tacoma, Washington, with Mitchell's close friend, bassist Red Kelly. A sixth, one Mitchell calls "a monster," looms on the horizon. That one he would like to station in Tokyo.

The basses are both a testament to Mitchell's love for the instrument and the jazz musician's mobility. Owning five basses has its practical aspects and reflects airline policies on bass fiddles. "Airlines don't want to see a bass being carried aboard a plane," Mitchell says. "They'll lose it or break it, or do anything else they can do to discourage you."

Red Mitchell hasn't always traveled by air, however. From 52nd Street, he went on the road with Jackie Paris, one of seven bands he was rehearsing with at the time. Another ensemble in rehearsal was one led by Miles Davis, but it was Paris who first got a gig. By the time Mitchell returned to New York eight weeks later, Miles had already recorded *Birth of the Cool*. It was one of those missed opportunities Mitchell plans to include in a book he jokingly says he'll title *The Greatest Things that Never Happened to Me*.

Work with Mundell Lowe and Charlie Ventura came next. Then, after a stint with Chubby Jackson's band, he did thirteen months of mostly grueling one-nighters with Woody Herman. The year was 1951.

Mitchell contracted tuberculosis and was forced to spend a year in treatment, rest, and recuperation.

But the following year he was out again, replacing Charles Mingus in vibraphonist Red Norvo's group on a tour that took him to Sweden with Billie Holiday. The tour package, organized by Leonard Feather, included, in addition to Norvo, Buddy DeFranco's Quartet and the Beryl Booker Trio. Billie Holiday carried only a piano player.

"They figured they would get a drummer and a bass player out of one of the groups," Mitchell says, "but it turned out I was the only one who wanted to play with her. Billie had a reputation—and she did—for telling it like it is. She had what I call the curse of absolute honesty, and not everybody is comfortable with that. Anyway, I just loved her. It was a great influence on me and I'm sure the others."

For Mitchell, the impact of Stockholm was just as lasting. "The first day we were here [Stockholm], Lady said, 'Take us to the slums. I want to see the slums.' The driver said there were no slums. Somebody else said there was no Beverly Hills either. I asked him if that was just Stockholm or all of Sweden? He said no, it's like that all over Sweden. I figured this must be the place. Anyway, I started following Sweden then, in the news, as a lot of people follow football or baseball teams, and it seemed like everything I saw made sense. I kind of smacked my forehead and said why doesn't everybody do that."

When Mitchell eventually left America permanently in 1968, it was not because of lack of work. He was still thinking about Sweden, and he suffered for his political activities. Nevertheless, he was firmly established in the Hollywood studios, and jazz gigs were much a part of his life. The studio scene, however, began to overshadow jazz. For Mitchell, there were choices to make, musically and politically.

"I didn't mind it when I first got into it," Mitchell says of studio work. "Barney Kessel recommended me for a film, *I Want to Live*, with Susan Hayward. Johnny Mandel had written the music and the band was Shelly Manne, Art Farmer, Bud Shank, Gerry Mulligan, Frank Rosalino, and Pete Jolly. That film was good; it was a message against the death penalty. In doing the film, they had built a replica of the gas chamber and we all took turns sitting in it. Boy, that was spooky.

"Then there were other things like the 'Peter Gunn Show.' At the time, that was the only detective show that used jazz, and Henry Mancini did the music. His writing for a chase scene was just Shelly and me playing, and I had to get down to low C somehow, so that led to tuning the bass in fifths. It was only logical to tune the bass to play all the music that's written for it. That part was exciting for me, a learning experience."

In 1959, when MGM was looking for a bassist, six composers specifically asked for Mitchell: Henry Mancini, Andre Previn, Johnny Mandel, George Stevens, Hugo Friedhoffer, and Pete Rugolo. "The contractor finally got it through his head," Mitchell says. "Six months before Ray Brown came to town I told him, if they ask for Ray, please don't say we've already got Red Mitchell. I got Ray on eventually, one picture, but it didn't really work all that well. You shouldn't have to be Ray Brown to get a studio gig. He's the real superman of the bass."

Keyboardist Artie Kane, who was first call pianist at both MGM and Fox—"which was against the rules"—became Mitchell's ally in an attempt to integrate the studio system. "We used to take on the music department, ask them questions like, 'How come the band is all white?' They'd ask if we knew anyone who was qualified and we'd give them all kinds of names. Plas Johnson, Red Callendar, Buddy Collette, Earl Palmer—they'd broken the color line in the studios. I really didn't think you should have to be that good to get a routine movie score. Artie asked Fox one time if they'd ever had a black composer. 'Why don't you try Quincy Jones,' Artie suggested. Quincy was already at Universal."

Politically, Mitchell was very active, and because of his beliefs he was uncomfortable with many of the films he was accompanying. "We used to discuss, does art really affect or influence reality? I think it goes both ways. The violence we were accompanying was influencing the violence on the street. We were taking the money and moaning all the way to the bank. At MGM I got time and a half and another fifty percent if I played fender, but it wasn't the quality of playing that counted, it was the flexibility. You were just supposed to say, no problem. But it was a great learning experience for me playing with all these legitimate bass players, learning from them."

Despite the number of movie and television dates Mitchell did in those days, jazz continued to be his guiding force. "I didn't consider myself a prostitute because I always put a good playing gig before a good paying gig. I always played the jazz gigs and got a sub for the studio dates if there was a conflict. I had that principle and I was almost alone in that.

"Toward the end, in 1968, when Martin Luther King was assassinated, I suggested we upset the system by disrupting the studio answering services. Those girls were getting about $100 a week. All of us could do a little nonviolent disruptive technique by asking, when we got a call, if the picture glorified violence. It just got a laugh at the bass club meeting; nobody thought it would work."

In 1966, Mitchell worked mostly with pianist Hampton Hawes. "I wouldn't have given that up for anything. Hampton and I opened Donte's for six weeks. They couldn't afford a drummer so it was just the two of us. I was going through the bass tuning process then and Hamp was extremely tolerant. I sent subs to the studio gigs during that period and the contractors didn't like it at all.

"By 1968, I was putting in so much time and energy in the studios that when I got to the jazz gigs I would be tired." Mitchell particularly remembers recording the score for *Doctor Zhivago*. "The guy wrote this one tune [Dr. Zhivago Theme] and we played it every day for six weeks. We were all going crazy." Mitchell also recalls a club date at Marty's on the Hill, with Oliver Nelson. "Most of the guys were studio players, so when a weekend TV thing came up I turned it down. Some of the guys didn't and as a result, the music suffered. The ethic then was, you took the good paying gigs, studio work, and tried to squeeze in jazz."

It was a musical philosophy Mitchell couldn't adhere to and in the end it cost him. "Harold Land and I had a quintet we were trying to keep together while I juggled studio dates. The most powerful contractor changed a date, and I said I couldn't come back that evening because of a rehearsal with Harold. He said, 'A rehearsal? If you do that you've blown it, I'll get somebody else for the rest of the year.' He did."

The real turning point for Mitchell musically, however, was having to refuse Dizzy Gillespie after an extended stay at the Lighthouse.

"I did six weeks with Dizzy. He loved the low C on the bass and he wanted me to stay with him and tour. I heard myself telling him, 'Diz, I've got this big house.' That's what I said. To pay for the house I've got to stay in the studios. Suddenly I thought, how did I get here from there? This is what I always wanted to do, play with Dizzy." Mitchell quit the studios.

There were no second thoughts about money he'd be giving up by moving to Europe. "None whatsoever," Mitchell said. "The last three months I didn't take any violent TV or movie dates. Instead I took a terrible wake up, happy TV show, 'Good Morning Los Angeles.' I decided to do that and just work clubs until I could get out. The Vietnam War was on, so they'd give the body count and then we were supposed to play 'It's a Wonderful World.' I went to the producer and told him we couldn't play that. So we compromised and played 'Softly as in a Morning Sunrise.'"

Mitchell also did some teaching during this period. "Once a week I would drive my son to this music school where he would take lessons. While he was doing that I would have a free bass class, which started with a request by Gerald Wiggins who wanted me to show his son J.J. something. This little bass course was kind of built around him. That went on for about two years. That was one of many things I was doing, trying to heal the wounds."

Mitchell's political activism eventually extended to the national level. Deeply distressed by the assassination of John F. Kennedy (who had earlier pardoned Hampton Hawes), Mitchell began to question the powers in office. He became involved in the NAACP, CORE, and everything in between. "I was doing benefits for the ACLU and then I was asked to hire the musicians and play at a club called Eugene's in Beverly Hills, for McCarthy. I was registered with the Peace and Freedom party, which was aligned with the Black Panthers. For three months they wanted me and finally I said I'll do it on one condition: if McCarthy will meet a friend of mine in the presence of qualified reporters."

Mitchell had in mind introducing McCarthy to the Jon Evans film made in the Oakland jail with Huey Newton, explaining what the Panthers were all about. "The first thing was to stop killing us. That stuff hadn't gotten out to the American people," Mitchell says of the film.

"By coincidence they [Newton and McCarthy] were using the same language but McCarthy's advisors were telling him to stay away from the race issue. The issue was never race, but racism, so he was not addressing black people, the jazz world, or me. Well, he was busy and it never happened until primary election night when they finally said okay. That was when we heard Bobby Kennedy was winning so we weren't going to go up there and be there while he [McCarthy] found out he lost. Then came the news that [Robert] Kennedy was killed. I almost puked; I just backed off and said don't heave, just leave."

By this time Mitchell began to think he was being watched. "In the States they were after me. I suppose anyone trying to get close to a presidential candidate was followed. I thought I was paranoid, but I wasn't." Mitchell's concern reached a level that caused him to seek out professional help. "In the last three months I went to a very highly paid shrink. She really helped me. Someday I'll get my FBI dossier, and if it isn't 500 pages I'll be drugged. Nothing communist, but you didn't have to do that to be followed in the sixties." Packing up his one bass, Mitchell left for Sweden.

A short time after his arrival in Stockholm, Mitchell had a reunion with some of the musicians he'd met in the fifties. The press interest was high and Mitchell consented to an interview against the advice of some of the musicians. "I did spill my guts to a reporter in 1968," Mitchell says. "The next day, although the reporter had not written the headline, it said: 'Rich Hollywood Musician Hops Off Sinking U.S.A.' "

For Mitchell, the moving to Europe question elicits a complex answer. "It seemed to me as though people would always ask me why I wanted to leave [America] and if I only had a few seconds I would say, 'It's the institutionalism of the violence and racism.' Okay, the country started with genocide and went on to slavery. In combination, I consider those birth defects problem number-one in America. I'd still like to help solve that problem; I tried to help in the sixties."

Despite those sentiments, Mitchell dislikes the expatriate label, and points out it's primarily one of language. "It sounds like someone who's lost his patriotism, but it's [expatriate] spelled with *iate* at the end, not *iot*, and expatriate only means one who's left his fatherland."

When Mitchell made the move to Europe, he had one gig—a month in Copenhagen. "That was exactly the kind of excuse I needed to get out of the studios. It was thirty-five dollars a night, but it was two weeks with Phil Woods and two weeks with Lucky Thompson. In Stockholm I had only one gig, a half-hour radio program played with a quartet organized by the head of the radio station, Bosse Broberg, who turned out to be one of my closest friends here and the fairest administrator I've ever worked for. He helped everybody.

"Over here [Sweden] I was treated as an individual. I got grants, and on one TV show I was told I was a national treasure. In general, the level of quality of Swedish musicians now is of the highest, very close to the U.S., but the mentality is definitely different. No matter how long you live in a country, you wind up realizing you're an American jazz musician living in Sweden. That's how people take me and that's who I am. Mark Murphy is right when he says you don't really know what it's like to be an American until you're out of the country."

Mitchell studied Swedish briefly and found almost no official problems. "Almost everybody speaks English. I knew that, but the first couple of years, I just listened, particularly to kids, studied Swedish for a few weeks, which is free, and if you are out of work you can go up to advanced literature. Residence permits were no problem except once and that was only a bureaucratic bungle. Rules are stiffer now though, especially for people from the Middle East and Eastern Europe. Their kind of racism here is about Swedes and non-Swedes. Like in Japan, you're either Japanese or you're not. I attribute a lot of it to the violent films but it's going on all over the world." Mitchell's response to this situation is characteristically musical. He writes songs about it, one called "Foreigner."

Mitchell found his presence in Stockholm caused no problem for local musicians. "In Stockholm? Almost none. For people who think categorically, I don't fit. Most promoters and club owners think either in terms of a foreign star coming in or a local guy, so I get left out of a lot of things—for ten years with one guy, and he had two clubs and a theater. All kinds of people came over and asked for me and were told I was busy, too expensive, out of town, and then they'd get mad at me for not showing up on the gig. It wasn't nationalism; I just didn't fit into the categories. Local guys, they thought Swedes; traveling guys, Americans. I was not a visiting star and I was not Swedish. I told everybody I was going to work for local money. They said it was a mistake, but I just wanted to play.

"I managed to avoid that once with Kai Winding [trombone]. I called the club owner all kinds of names and told him the first time I work for you it's going to be for foreign money. The following year he started the jazz festival and all was okay, good money. There's a jazz club funded by city and state which makes all its money on visiting stars. I've worked there like three nights on a good year."

For nearly eight years, Mitchell was content, enjoying life in Sweden and playing jazz. Then, in December 1975, he made his first return trip to America. "I missed the Nixon years," Mitchell says. "We went to the West Coast, hung out with Red Kelly, then Mill Valley with Jon Hendricks, then L.A. with Red Callendar. It was a great month. The red carpet was out, everybody was saying welcome back. I even worked New Year's Eve with Jack Sheldon. I had a lot of thoughts about moving back [to the United States] then, especially when I got back to Sweden and the government did that thing to Ingmar Bergman.

"The tax department had him busted during a rehearsal for back taxes. They had TV cameras outside the stage door, but they broke him down. It took him two months to recover. That put me through a crisis; this was what I thought I was getting away from."

Mitchell did learn about the quota system in Paris, an experience many musicians had in that city that called for a specified number of French musicians for every foreign one. "We got fired," Mitchell says, "me and two Swedish musicians for violating the quota law. For two weeks it went really well, but when they wanted to hold us over for ten days, I couldn't find replacements in Paris. The club owner took a chance sending for the Swedish guys. We played three nights, then this really arrogant, blind tenor player wanted to sit in. I said no, we're playing our own stuff now. We were fired the next day. This guy was very big with the union so we had a week off in Paris with no pay but we did do a record and a TV show. In England in the early fifties Ray Brown couldn't play behind Ella. Ray could only be the conductor. Our own musicians' union has to share the blame for that because it's a bitch bringing someone to the U.S."

Working with Swedish musicians, who Mitchell says are vastly improved now, is the same as anywhere in the world. "Right away when you think of drummers you think of Art Blakey, but there was only one of him. I worked with Kenny Drew [piano] and Tootie Heath [drums] when I first came over. Tootie had lived here for awhile and he told me about the drummers. 'One gets all the work and you're going to love the other one.'"

Sweden also provided Mitchell with the opportunity to pursue an old ambition—songwriting. "I kind of promised myself I wanted to improvise words and music at the same time. I knew it could be done. I had fooled around with it from the time I was kid and used songwriting as a rest camp on the way to that. I won two Swedish Grammys over here with my own tunes but distribution is the bottleneck." In 1986 *Home Suite* won a Grammy, and *A Declaration of Interdependence* won a Grammy for 1990.

When Red's friend, guitarist Jim Hall, came over to hang out and talk about the two of them working together in New York, Mitchell started making trips back. "We worked Sweet Basil's, Japan, all around the country but mostly at Bradley's. That started my going back regularly to New York."

Did Mitchell's thinking about music extend even to the proliferation of rock musicians making enormous amounts of money? "One thought about that, my rationalization that gets me through is, I had a relationship with a bass company through Monk Montgomery. During that term, I really found out. I met the guy who had developed all that stuff—guitars, basses, amps. I found out that they weren't just selling millions of guitars, but tens of millions.

"The odds, if there are 100 million players, they're not all going to get a gig. Let's say they all learn three chords. They're always going to identify as players. When they suddenly one day hear there are four or five chords we [jazz] might get five percent more people for jazz audiences. Eventually they'll hear more than three chords. It's like Jim Hall and I going to hear Segovia. There's also a new wave of interest in standards led by people like Harry Connick, Jr. People are finally realizing the standards are with us to stay. They'll be around as long as Mozart. I think the general population is finally starting to really hear jazz. I hope I'm not wrong."

If Mitchell missed anything about America it was, as might be expected, the common experiences, the American informality, the American jazz radio stations. "People don't just drop by here, but living here helped me as a musician. It probably saved my life. Jazz musicians are more respected here than they are in the States. I've spoken about that a lot of times. It has to do with the youth of our country, it's only two hundred years old. American people in general, at least so far—we'll see what happens—seem to be embarrassed about using the word *soul*. They don't think they have one, they don't know what it is. They don't seem to realize the American soul is expressed by this music that we play—jazz. It's loved all over the world. It's won hearts and minds that American politics have not won. There's an enormous rise in chauvinism all over the world. I hope it happens in America, that the government gets chauvinistic about its artists. It's finally happening even in Sweden."

In 1977, Mitchell toured Japan with Jim Hall and Art Farmer and immediately became a convert. Drummer Donald Bailey was already living there and completed the quartet. "They [Japanese] lost World War II but they never lost their dignity. They took a step back and said what did we do wrong? They finally realized what America offered was baseball, technology, and jazz. One of my songs is called 'Emulate the Japanese.' I did a record there once with Donald Bailey and some Japanese musicians. A saxophonist, who was after Bird, came pretty close. When I asked him to play an intro by himself, he said, 'What should I play?' I said, 'You're free to play anything you like.' He said, 'Free?' and then sounded just like Ornette Coleman."

Mitchell has his own group, but continues to work mostly with other people. "I do have a trio, a piano player and a tenor player who just toured the States, but we ran into some bureaucratic bullshit. We made a record I really like." Partly for economic reasons and partly because he likes working at Bradley's in New York, Mitchell has become something of a duo specialist, working and recording with pianists such as Kenny Baron, Hank Jones, Jimmy Rowles, and Bill Mays.

"There's something about the number two," Mitchell said in a 1989 interview with Lee Hildebrand of the *San Francisco Chronicle.* "It's like the smallest possible society. It's a matter of being both selfish and groupish at the same time. I think a functioning jazz group is a perfect example of how people can come together with love and be both groupish and selfish at the same time."

Another facet of Mitchell's life is his Communication Seminar, which he teaches primarily through playing jazz. "There are three parts: within ourselves, the lust to play jazz; among us on the stand and buses, classes; backstage, with the rest of the world and even in some ways with the universe. It's an attempt to eliminate the usual breakdowns in communications. That's how I start. I would never try to explain that magic moment when it really happens, when the forces of nature are flowing through you." The seminars began in Denmark but Mitchell has given them all over the world. Three have been given at meetings of The International Society of Bassists. In January 1992, Mitchell presented one at the International Association of Jazz Educators in Miami, Florida.

In the spring of 1992, after twenty-four years abroad, Mitchell decided to return home. "All seriousness aside I miss the jazz scene in New York, but it's out of the question for me to live there. It's necessary to commute, but now it makes more sense to do that from Salem, Oregon [his destination], than come from here [Stockholm]. For me, it makes more sense to live there and commute to Europe once a year."

If the past is any indicator, Mitchell will probably continue to pursue his political and socially conscious activities. He penned an open letter to the then general secretary of the Soviet Union, Mikhail Gorbachev. The letter appeared in Gene Lees's *Jazz Newsletter*, the *Polish Jazz Forum*, and a Swedish publication. In it, Mitchell pledged his support for peace, argued for nuclear disarmament, and a world political system.

Mitchell's perspective, after one of the longest exile periods, is clear and he speaks for many musicians when he says, "By doing what we've done, in my case for twenty-four years, we've definitely taken ourselves out of the limelight. There are a lot of people who think we're dead. We have nothing to kick about, not being at the center of the stage."

Perhaps the same is true for Mitchell as for guitarist Jimmy Raney, who told Mitchell, "I've become a living legend—forgotten but not gone."

—January 1992

Eleven months after this interview, Red Mitchell died in Salem, Oregon.

15

*Japanese jazz fans?
They knew more about
me than I knew about
myself.*
– Donald 'Duck' Bailey

Donald 'Duck' Bailey

One of the first lessons drummer Donald Bailey learned when he arrived in Japan was the way the Japanese do business, even in jazz. "If they want you for a gig, it's not just a phone call," says Bailey. "They invite you out to dinner first, like we do here with other businesses, which is pretty nice. It puts things on a different level. It's all first class. It makes a big difference. You wonder why it's not done like that here. You're also paid well in Japan, which is another side of the story. They know you're not paid well in this country so they pay well and hope you'll come back."

Bailey not only went back, he stayed. After an initial tour with Peggy Lee, he listened to some producers, liked what he heard, and took up residence in Tokyo. When he returned to America five years later, in 1982, Bailey felt he had changed considerably because of the experience.

"It took me time to get adjusted," Bailey says. "I was kind of angry about being an American. It was something in me but after that I developed. They understood me more than I did them. They kind of cooled me out. Living in Japan changed my thinking a lot."

Born in Philadelphia, "Duck," as he has been known since childhood, is largely a self-taught musician. Although known primarily as a drummer, he also plays harmonica, piano, baritone saxophone, and trombone. After free-lancing around Philadelphia, he joined organist Jimmy Smith in 1956, and for the next eight years, he toured and recorded with Smith.

In the mid sixties, Bailey moved to Los Angeles and worked with such musicians as Harold Land, Bobby Bryant, Mundell Lowe, and pianist Hampton Hawes. Bailey is the quintessential sideman on hundreds of recordings, an in-demand drummer noted for his light touch and precise time. Other instruments, however, have always held great interest for him—most notably the harmonica.

He received some unexpected help from one of the masters of the harmonica, Jean "Toots" Thielmans. "I was playing with Jimmy Smith, when Toots came to the Showboat in Philly," Bailey says. "I'd heard him on record. Stan Getz was there too, kind of puttin' him on. Then he [Toots] got up there and just ripped it apart. I asked him a question and he gave me some pointers. The harmonica is not played from the diaphragm, but from the throat, that's how you get your speed."

Bailey's harmonica was one of three heard on the sound track for the film *Buck and the Preacher*, starring Harry Belafonte and Sidney Poitier. "I got this call," Bailey says, "from, I think it was, Benny Carter. There was one part he wanted me to play like Sonny Terry. As soon as he said that, I knew I couldn't do it. With those guys, the language comes through their instrument. We tried, but finally they flew Terry in. He walked into that studio, sat down and put the harmonica in his mouth, and it was all over. We all just shook our heads."

Arriving in Japan with Peggy Lee, Bailey found he was already well known to Japanese jazz fans, primarily from his recordings with Jimmy Smith. "They knew more about me than I knew about myself," Bailey says. "They bring out that part of you that's needed. It's not exactly an ego thing, but it made it very comfortable for me to be there. They were very good audiences. They seemed to have a different feeling about the music. I didn't want to come home."

During Bailey's stay in Japan, his work was largely at small jazz clubs. "There were a lot of them in the Repongi District," Bailey says. "They didn't always last but they sprung up everywhere. A couple, like Misty's and Body and Soul, were very stable. There are also still a number of jazz coffee houses, equipped with state-of-the-art sound systems and large jazz record collections, where you can order an album with your coffee."

For Bailey, there were also the occasional tours with other visiting American musicians. Art Farmer, Kenny Burrell, Red Mitchell, Jackie McLean, Mal Waldron, and Jim Hall were some of the musicians Bailey played with. The bulk of his work, however, was with Japanese musicians.

He recorded over fifty albums during his stay, including one with George Kawaguchi, a drum star for years, and a ten-year-old drum prodigy whom Bailey had taught briefly. Bailey says the youngster "could imitate Max [Roach] and Philly [Joe Jones] and then want to go play marbles." Most of those recordings Bailey made in Japan are not available in this country. "I found one at Tower Records," Bailey says, "where I was leader and playing harmonica."

"There was a tremendous amount of work," Bailey says. "Japan is the only place I've been overworked, and there was no resentment from Japanese musicians. I have no complaints about that. They were very cordial, very nice, and happy to work with me." There were also opportunities for informal teaching, although Bailey says he might have done more if he had spoken Japanese. "I just told guys to come by my gig, listen to me play, and take what they wanted."

If there were any musical adjustments to make, they were ones of feel or beat in the rhythm sections. "They had a different type of beat, time feeling, and it was difficult for me to adjust to at first. I felt more comfortable eventually. It's like the difference between swing or bebop and today's music," Bailey says. "The music is more on top now, the groove being on two and four." [1]

Whenever he was reunited with visiting Americans, Bailey noticed the difference even more. "I'd think, yeah, this is where it really is. When it was somebody from my era I'd think, why does this feel so good? You lock into that. I think I can play with anybody as long as they have good time, if they know where one is. At one time, I remember I didn't feel right playing with people that didn't sound like Bud Powell or Bird. In Japan I heard a different type of expression. They were just playing jazz with a different feeling."

Personally, Bailey counts his Japanese experience as very rewarding, particularly regarding the race question. Unlike musicians in Paris or Stockholm or Copenhagen, there was no colony of Americans in Tokyo to keep in touch with. "I was just aware that there weren't any [Americans] around," Bailey says. "There was one guy I met who had a restaurant. I used to visit him. I was the only black face but I still felt so at home. There are certain things you need to be whole. Japan was the first place I went I didn't feel like I was black. There was not one problem. Maybe if you went to the suburbs where they haven't seen black people, they might glance at you, but there was no undercurrent of prejudice. I was just a person and knowing that changes your whole being. They made me feel great. I was just treated very well with a lot of respect. Maybe it has something to do with their religion being different from ours."

With lots of work, friends, and an atmosphere conducive to growing as a musician and a person, Bailey missed little about the States. "I don't think I missed anything. I was busy learning how to deal with the changes, the culture. I learned a lot of patience. There are so many people over there, seeing how they dealt with situations was very important."

Bailey recalls no exceptional amount of jazz on radio or Japanese television, but there was one program that surprised him: a thirty-minute film about his life story. "I was really taken by surprise that they would take that much interest in a sideman," Bailey says. "It would never have happened here [United States]. You have to be a big star to get even a little bit of that here."

Given the Japanese zeal for jazz, it's perhaps not unusual. "Doctors, actors, important people in society looked on jazz as a high form of music. Japanese musicians don't understand why it's not like that here. A lot of guys would tell me they were saving their money, going to the States, and I'd tell them, don't be surprised if this music is not around like you might think."

While Bailey didn't study Japanese formally, he did learn a lot about the Japanese way of life and philosophy, particularly when he attempted to remedy an official matter himself. It was an experience that perhaps has political implications. "I forgot that in Japan when somebody tells you something it just means they're going to try, not that they're going to do it. When I look at the present administration, they're not aware of this. American politicians go to Japan and try to make deals and are told yes. That only means they [the Japanese] will try it. It means they're only thinking about it. It never really means yes. All these statesmen, politicians, don't seem to realize that. A lie over there is not like a lie here. *Uso* they call it. It's not heavy. The reality is something else and yet when we hear it, we're disturbed. That's why it's so important to learn that cultures are different."

Bailey's explanation for Japan's high interest in jazz is study and a high regard for history. "I think they study and learn about cultures, more of the truth about how things got started, especially music. They learned the truth about jazz. Here, we don't do that. They do it in schools, through the media. People who like jazz can see it, hear it, study it, talk about it. You see posters about jazz on busses over there. Older musicians work more than here. When they're not on the scene as much, they're passing on the information to younger musicians. There are lots of drum schools over there with hundreds of students. They treat jazz as a high-class art form. They know, they really know about jazz."

Bailey returned to America in 1982. After free-lancing around Los Angeles for a year he joined singer Carmen McRae. "That was an experience," Bailey says. "Carmen can be difficult. She's hard on drummers, but I learned a lot about dynamics from her." Bailey toured Europe with McRae and also made some return trips to Japan before leaving the road and settling in Oakland, California, with wife Susie Laraine. A saxophonist, Laraine is part of a group called Five Winged Birds, an all-female saxophone quintet devoted to the music of Charlie Parker.

Bailey continues his free-lance recording work with such musicians as Jimmy Rowles, Red Mitchell, Ray Brown, and the group Bebop and Beyond, featuring Dizzy Gillespie. Another recording with saxophonists Pete Christlieb and Bob Cooper was released in 1991.

Bailey continues to explore other instruments in a group he calls The Other Side. In this group, in addition to drums, he plays harmonica, piano, saxophone, and trombone. Another of Bailey's groups is an octet called 8 Misbehavin'. Bailey hopes to record this group.

Teaching privately takes up some of his time, and he also runs a twice weekly jazz workshop open to older and young musicians alike and designed to revive the jam session atmosphere. "It's very rewarding musically, and something I feel I have to do. Jazz has given me a lot so I have to give it back," Bailey says.

As a part of the jazz scene for over thirty years, Bailey sees the current trend of younger musicians returning to jazz roots and acoustic sound as a positive step and is especially pleased with the efforts of musicians such as Wynton Marsalis, who Bailey cites for his efforts at jazz education. "Black people are less educated about jazz. When he [Marsalis] comes out, I see him want to open up, he wants people to get educated. Young musicians want to be like this guy. But it'll never happen here in the States; I can't be optimistic. I see it getting worse. Jazz seems like background music. There's no appreciation except in special clubs. I don't think they really know where jazz is."

Bailey has some reservations about Marsalis and the new breed of jazz musician, however, and it's simply one of paying dues. "It [their music] might lack the expression from learning it the hard way. I can always hear a certain 'cry of acceptance' in Bird or Miles or Jackie McLean. There was a cry there that said, please accept me. That produced a certain kind of feeling, like, 'Hey, man, accept me, look what I can do.' There's a lot of that feeling that's not there now. He [Marsalis] plays but that cry is not there; he hasn't struggled, although it's not his fault.

"Environment plays a lot as to what you become. You're hungry, you're going to try harder, exert more of yourself. That struggle part of it is missing for me. Not feeling accepted for myself in this country, I wanted to prove myself with my drums if that was the only way I could do it. Like those blues players, that was all they could do so that feeling really came out."

Bailey has no quarrel with the rock scene, nor electronics if it's used musically. He does find it puzzling, however, when people of position and power, who were jazz artists themselves, fail to do much for the music. Radio and television exposure is vital, Bailey feels. "Young people will go any direction they hear on the radio or see on TV. Jazz could happen again with that kind of exposure. A lot of times we hurt ourselves. But you can't blame a person for being allowed to be made a star. I don't blame them at all. Miles probably said, 'This is too hard, I'm going up.' But this system doesn't push the mentors out there, the older musicians. Give them grants, set them up someplace, let them teach. I wish it would be some of the deep guys. The last thing they want to do is support something like jazz."[2]

The memory and lesson of Japan is still deeply felt by Bailey. "Guys coming over would ask me about coming back. There was no reason to come home. In a sense I think I learned a lot about culture. When I came back to this country, I could see that there was a big change in me. I don't think I was the same person. I learned how to deal with people, tolerate different styles, the way that they feel their music. Other people have different feelings, different time, and it's still okay."

Given Bailey's positive experience in Japan, one wonders why he didn't stay longer. But there were official problems that simply couldn't be worked out. "I wish I was back there now, to be blunt about it. I would have stayed, never come back. I was in a position to be booking acts from the States. I had a place to work, play jazz. I saw that building up.

"I would rather be over there and live as a human being and be appreciated as a jazz musician. I had more friends over there than I ever had in my life. The respect they give musicians, art itself, they at least attempt to put it out so performers can feel this respect. In this country, it'll be a long while before we get there."

—Oakland, California, 1992

*Do you know how
many Europeans learn
English just so they can
take up jazz?
– Walter Norris*

Coda

When Bud Freeman returned to America in 1980, it was, by his own admission, a journey filled with trepidation and doubt. After six years in London, going back, even at the request of the mayor of Chicago, guaranteed nothing. Freeman's doubts, however, were unwarranted. His homecoming was marked by a warm reception at the Chicago Heritage Jazz Festival, and much to his surprise, he had not been forgotten. At age eighty, he continued to tour, as his health allowed, mostly in the Midwest, and also combined his performances with anecdotal lectures.

In 1985, a tour of New England included a story session with Harvard undergraduates, and the same year saw the release of a new album, *The Real Bud Freeman*. By then, Freeman was not surprised at his reception. With characteristic humor, he maintained that musicians his age "can still command audiences because they just want to see if we can pick up a horn without falling down."[1] Shortly before his death in 1991, Freeman's third book, *Crazeology*, was published. In Japan, however, Freeman would no doubt have been regarded as a national treasure, and in his later years he wouldn't have been forced to continue enduring the rigors of the road.

In addition to Freeman, there are other bright spots on the jazz horizon for exiles. Johnny Griffin is working often in the United States again, as is Art Farmer, who has been coming back to record and tour for several years. Mal Waldron, Billie Holiday's accompanist for the last two years of her life, has made a number of trips back for recording and concert appearances.

Trumpeter Benny Bailey, who got his first taste of Europe in 1948 with Dizzy Gillespie, returned home in the eighties after twenty-seven years abroad. Bailey became a member of Harry Arnold's band in Stockholm, which, unlike other radio bands, was totally devoted to jazz.

"I'm glad I went," Bailey said. "I was able to maintain my individuality over there because I was not forced to play whatever was current in order to make a living."

Saxophonist Sahib Shihab's experience in Europe was similar to Bailey's. Shihab also returned in the early eighties after nearly twenty-five years in Denmark and Sweden. He departed for Europe in 1959,

Dexter Gordon (Ken Whitten Collection)

Shihab said, "for survival and peace of mind. I had begun to lose faith in mankind. I also wanted to find out where I was coming from musically."

The most notable returnee, however, was saxophonist Dexter Gordon, whose feature role in the film *'Round Midnight* focused attention on the exile life and jazz in a way that had never been done before. Unlike most other jazz films, authenticity was the guiding force in the conception of *'Round Midnight*. In addition to Gordon, other musicians were used for the principal roles, and Gordon himself had considerable input on the script.

"When we had divergent views, Dexter was very helpful in giving us insight and so were other musicians, such as saxophonist Wayne

Shorter," says cowriter and director Bertrand Tavernier. "I always discussed the meaning of their lines with them, checking to see if they rang true."

Such attention to detail is laudable, especially when compared with Hollywood's previous attempts to depict the jazz life. *Young Man with a Horn,* loosely based on the life of trumpeter Bix Beiderbecke; *The Gene Krupa Story*; and *Lady Sings the Blues,* a grossly distorted version of Billie Holiday's life, immediately come to mind. By contrast, *'Round Midnight* is a substantially accurate picture of the Paris jazz scene in the sixties. It perhaps comes as no surprise, however, that the film was done by a French director.

Tavernier's approach clearly reflects not only the French attitude toward jazz, but that of Europe in general. Tavernier's reverence for jazz at least partially explains why so many American musicians opted for a life of exile. "To me, bebop musicians are the real geniuses of America, the continuation of Debussy, Fauré, Bartok, and Ravel. They created the only music in America that has never been co-opted or bastardized by the system. Duke Ellington's purity was usurped by Broadway when they did a white version of *Sophisticated Ladies.* But bebop has never been tampered with. Nobody can do it because bebop is such a free music. Thelonious Monk used to say if you understand the meaning of bebop, you understand the meaning of freedom. I tried to reflect this spirit in the structure of the film; no intricate plot, no twists, but a free flow with voice overs, time lapses, and the laying of one musical number over another. Dizzy Gillespie said, 'Bebop is the most serious music ever made in America, and a lot of people died for it.' And as Dexter reminded me, bebop is such a light name for such a demanding music."[2]

In *'Round Midnight,* Gordon portrays a character composite of Bud Powell and Lester Young, though he admitted, "there must have been a hundred personalities in him." Keenly aware of the responsibility and opportunity at last to make an authentic jazz film, Gordon agonized over his portrayal. "It was twenty-four hours a day. Wake up in the middle of the night and sit on the bed thinking. Because I wanted it so much to be real. I felt like I represented all these hundreds of cats. Not that they'd all been to Europe, but they were all jazz musicians who had paid their dues and got no admiration and got no remuneration. And somehow I grasped the reality of that."[3]

The film was given a good deal of media attention with reviews and major articles in *The New York Times* and *New York Magazine* as well as the expected coverage in various jazz publications. With the film's general distribution, and Gordon's Academy Award nomination, the public was made aware of a period of jazz history previously unknown to them.

'Round Midnight was followed by the Clint Eastwood film *Bird* (1989), which one critic called "the first film about jazz by somebody who likes jazz." Eastwood treated the subject matter accordingly. The script, based on the unpublished *Life in E-Flat* by Chan Parker, was scored by using original Parker solos superimposed over a newly recorded rhythm section sound track. While many people were disappointed because they felt the film focused too heavily on Parker's drug problems, *Bird* opened new doors for jazz in film and set new standards.

Bruce Weber's film of Chet Baker, *Let's Get Lost*, shed new light on this trumpeter's troubled life. A film documentary on Thelonious Monk, *Straight, No Chaser*, by Charlotte Zwerin and Bruce Ricker, was also a welcome addition to jazz literature. Spike Lee's film *Mo' Better Blues* (1990) again focused on jazz but fell far short of its intent. Nevertheless, the film brought jazz before the public at a time when jazz was experiencing boosts from several unexpected fronts.

A cigarette company set an example for corporate America when it financed a recording and world tour of an all-star band led by pianist Gene Harris. Andrew Whist, president of the Philip Morris Jazz Grant, said of his company's involvement, "It is our view that jazz never received the corporate and national support it merits as art and music. There is ample room for other corporate and national initiatives—we have barely scratched the surface." On other fronts, Yves Saint Laurent unveiled a fragrance called Jazz. Drummer Max Roach received a MacArthur Foundation Genius Grant of $375,000, and Congressman John Conyers of Michigan succeeded in proposing and passing legislation that will make jazz a national treasure.

On the jazz education front, more of the masters are being uti-

Slide Hampton (Photo by Grant Collingwood, Ken Whitten Collection)

lized in jazz studies programs. Max Roach, David Baker, Nathan Davis, Jackie McLean, and Don Menza, for example, are to be found on American university campuses. And Paul H. Jeffrey, who heads the jazz studies program at Duke University, worked hard to bring the Thelonious Monk Institute to Durham, North Carolina.

Despite the appearance of jazz films, and other examples of jazz moving into the mainstream of American culture, the music continues to be shouldered aside by rock and other popular music forms. But there are signs of improvement, and in some cases the jazz community is speaking up.

During the 1985 Grammy awards ceremonies, a nationally televised event, all the jazz category awards were presented off camera. Musicians and critics alike were so incensed that they mounted a major protest, and in 1986 and 1987, jazz artists were given on-camera exposure, as well as several feature numbers. Most notable was Bobby McFerrin singing the title song from 'Round Midnight on the 1987 telecast.

With the advent of such jazz-oriented groups as Spyro Gyra appearing at major U.S. jazz festivals, audiences are being exposed to the more sophisticated jazz harmonies, and as a result they are exploring and expanding their listening tastes. The return of Miles Davis from a long illness and forced retirement also brought new fans into the jazz fold. Davis's musical policy of jazz-oriented rock pained jazz purists, but this former 52nd Street pioneer nevertheless made many new fans who are becoming increasingly aware of the importance of jazz to the development of rock. Davis and a number of other jazz artists even made videos that are occasionally seen on MTV. Before his death in 1991, Davis collaborated with Michel Legrand on the sound track for the movie *Dingo*.

Another factor in the return of many of the exiles is the youthful renaissance of mainstream jazz led by trumpeter Wynton Marsalis. "Young men can now make a living playing straight ahead jazz, and Wynton is responsible for that being possible," says Don Morgenstern, director of the Institute of Jazz Studies at Rutgers University.[4]

With New Orleans roots, and a musical family, Marsalis earned his spurs with Art Blakey's Jazz Messengers. He's since won Grammys in both jazz and classical categories, and inspired such musicians as Marcus Roberts, Chris Hollyday, Mark Whitfield, Renee Rosnes, the Harper Brothers, Joey DeFrancisco, Terrance Blanchard, and Roy Hargrove. These and other younger musicians have brought about a new jazz age, a return to acoustic sound, one that bodes well for many of the jazz exiles.

It's a state of affairs that has also made record companies happy. With jazz productions costing less than rock—$25,000 to $85,000 versus $150,000 plus—profits are now possible with jazz sales as low as thirty thousand copies.[5]

There is, however, a catch to this jazz renaissance. After being shouldered aside by rock and sent packing to Europe, the older musicians, many of them former exiles, now find themselves in the curious position of being replaced by younger versions of themselves. Some are not happy about it. "They're getting a place in jazz history that they have not deserved or earned," says bassist Ron Carter. Veteran musicians also complain that record companies, jumping on the youth movement bandwagon, are passing them over for the younger players.[6]

Marsalis, however, is acutely aware of the lessons of his elders and passes on the message wherever he goes, pointing to Duke Ellington as the jazzman who best embodied the mythology of this country in his music.

A resurgence of jazz on television through PBS and Arts and Entertainment cable outlets, should also be noted. Major features on Duke Ellington, Sarah Vaughan, Art Blakey, Charlie Parker, and Louis Armstrong have been a part of the American Masters Series. Billy Taylor's regular jazz features on "CBS Sunday Morning" are a welcome addition to network television, exposing some previously unheralded jazz veterans to a mass audience. Another bright spot is the appointment of Branford Marsalis to the "Tonight Show." Jazz on American television is still meager when compared with the exposure on European television, however.

On radio, National Public Radio (NPR) and university stations such as KLON-FM in Long Beach, California, continue to lead in presenting jazz; but as yet, jazz on commercial stations is extremely rare, and nothing like the variety of jazz programing found, for example, on the BBC in England can be cited in America. One such program that ran for some time was called "Jazz Score." A panel of prominent musicians tried to identify soloists, singers, or bands from records, and in the process, shared anecdotes from the jazz life.

The publishing industry continues to be wary of jazz books, despite the apparent proliferation of jazz publications, but there are new and important biographies of major jazz figures. At the other end of the spectrum, however, Ross Russell's biography of Charlie Parker remains out of print in this country, and saxophonist Art Pepper's hardcover autobiography, *Straight Life*, went out of print less than a year after its publication. In Japan it was a best seller.

Downbeat magazine, once the bible of jazz, has undergone major editorial changes and is now filled more with rock news and artist profiles than jazz. Only the Maryland-based *Jazz Times* continues with major jazz coverage; but again, one of the leading jazz publications in the world is Japan's *Swing Journal*, a prime example of the Japanese reverence for jazz that is second only to Europe's.

With the return and rejuvenation enjoyed by many exiles, one can only speculate on what would have happened had Charlie Parker or Billie Holiday gone to Europe and become exiles. Some musicians suggest Parker or Holiday might be alive today had they gone to Europe. As longtime exile Kenny Clarke told Parker, "Bird, you're slowly and surely committing suicide in America. Come over here and *live*. Here you will be treated as an artist—the French understand these things."[7] While Clarke took his own advice and remained in Europe until his death in 1985, Parker did not and suffered much the same fate as Bud Powell and Billie Holiday. Parker lost his cabaret card over narcotics charges and, in the cruelest of ironies, was banned from playing at Birdland, the club that had been named for him.

Pianist Bud Powell's problems stemmed largely from his treatment at the hands of the Philadelphia police. An alcoholic, and an occasional patient in mental institutions, Powell was beaten severely. By the time he went to Paris in 1959, the damage was done. Befriended by sympathetic Frenchmen, some of his musical brilliance was re-

Bud Powell (Ken Whitten Collection)

captured, but he contracted tuberculosis, resumed drinking, and slid back into madness before his death in 1964.

Singer Billie Holiday was made to suffer, among other things, the indignity of having to use the freight elevator in the United States even when she was the featured vocalist with Artie Shaw. Mal Waldron, recalling a 1958 European tour, says, "By the end of the year we returned to America, which I think is why Billie died. If she had stayed in Europe she'd probably be alive today."[8]

Despite the success of returning exiles and the resurgence of mainstream jazz by a cadre of young musicians returning to jazz roots, the feeling persists among many musicians that Europe remains the better climate for jazz. For those musicians, there *is* someplace like home. Waldron, a European resident since 1965, returns for an occasional visit or recording session but remains a staunch supporter of the exile life.

"In America, the artist is considered low man on the totem pole— which puts me underneath the ground." Waldron—as did Phil Woods, Donald Bailey, and Art Farmer—discovered through touring, another haven for jazz: the Far East. "Japan," Waldron says, "is the jazzman's paradise. They read every piece of literature they can find about jazz musicians, they know every record you've ever made. It's a real ego trip to go to Japan. You have to sign autographs for two hours after a gig."

Phil Woods agrees. "Oh, I'm hot as a two-dollar pistol in Japan. Japan is extremely avid for jazz. It's the second biggest record market, period. Per capita, it's the most literate country in the world; they read more books than anybody. I love touring in Japan. It's difficult— you do a lot of one-nighters, but their audiences are something else, man, and the people who take care of you, who present you! You don't have to scuffle. First class all the way, man. Always first class."[9]

Pianist Kenny Drew echoes those views about Japan. Drew enjoys an exclusive record affiliation of his own with RCA Victor, Japan. His records sell anywhere from forty thousand to sixty thousand copies— almost unheard-of numbers for a jazz artist—and in 1984 Drew became the second musician to be awarded the special prize of Japan's *Swing Journal*. The first musician accorded this honor was Duke Ellington. "I still love New York," says Drew, "give or take a few things, but my life is in Europe. I wouldn't want to live in the States again— too much upheaval. But I remain one hundred percent American."[10]

So does fluegelhornist Art Farmer, who settled in Vienna in 1968, both for the musical opportunities and the way of life. "I'm in Vienna about a third of the year, and the rest of the time, I'm on the road—in

Kenny Drew (Photo by Grant Collingwood, Ken Whitten Collection)

Europe, in the United States, in Japan. I'm very well known here, and I feel I have the respect of the people." [11]

Pianist Walter Norris agrees with Farmer. A resident of West Berlin since 1977, Norris remains in Europe primarily for musical considerations. Before his appointment as guest professor at the Hochschule der Kunste, Norris was pianist for the Sender Freis Berlin, a radio studio orchestra.

"I knew the job would include improvising as well as playing everything that was put in front of me. I knew the pay was good, I also knew

I would have a first-rate concert grand to work on and one of the world's best piano technicians to take care of it. What I didn't know was that I would also have at my disposal a two-meter Bosendorfer piano and a private locked room to use it in."

Norris hopes to establish a jazz program at the Hochschule, but admits the pull of New York is strong. "New York, in particular, wakes up the musical vibrations in the jazz animal. I remember that about New York when I'm not there and it sustains me. Jazz should be far more widely accepted in the world than it is. Do you know how many Europeans learn English just so they can take up jazz?"[12]

Soprano saxophonist Steve Lacy, who often teamed with Mal Waldron, remains in Paris where he has lived since 1970. Having worked in a variety of musical styles—Monk, Cecil Taylor—Lacy was originally inspired by the first of the jazz exiles, Sidney Bechet, and began playing soprano before John Coltrane. He returns home occasionally for work and recording, and during his two decades in Europe, he has emerged as a prolific composer.

"I was writing music like I'm writing now," Lacy said in an interview with Francis Davis, "but I couldn't find anyone to play it." Lacy gravitated to Paris because he knew he'd find good musicians there. Lacy's experience as an American in Paris is more like that of the American novelists and painters than fellow musicians. "It was that other stuff that attracted me too—all the arts with a capital A. I like to rub up against it." But finding an audience in Paris can be just as difficult as in New York. Comparing his jazz to the visual arts, Lacy says, "You're considered a failure if you have an empty gallery in New York. In Paris you're not."

Race did not play a part in Lacy's expatriation, except indirectly. Lacy is white but some of his musicians are black. To return home on Lacy's conditions would mean, "You'd have to uproot my band, and my drummer and piano player might not want to come."[13]

Lacy's fortunes brightened considerably in 1992 when he was named a recipient of a John D. and Catherine T. MacArthur genius grant, a $340,000 no-strings-attached award given over the next five years.

Leo Wright and Carmel Jones continued on staff with the Berlin

Radio. Jones has since returned to America and Wright died in 1990. Herb Geller is still firmly entrenched with Radio Hamburg, and pianist Horace Parlan remains in Denmark, as does drummer Ed Thigpen, whose most celebrated work was with Oscar Peterson and Ella Fitzgerald. Since moving to Denmark in 1972, Thigpen has combined a performing career with education. He does clinics for Remo drums and Sabian Cymbals, as well as teaching for the Danish Conservatory for Jazz and Latin American music.

Scores of musicians remain scattered around Europe, coming together periodically with their peers from home for festivals and concerts, while preferring the more relaxed life away from the New York struggle.

Trumpeter-arranger Thad Jones, who briefly took over the reins of the Count Basie Band, returned to Copenhagen early in 1986 but died only a few months later. After lengthy stays abroad, he found, as Johnny Griffin did, that returning home is not always the best idea.

"I played the same halls as Arthur Rubinstein in Europe," says Griffin. "The people who operated those halls had respect for us as musicians. At Carnegie Hall in New York, for example, the people seem to hate jazz musicians. The stagehands do everything they can to make life unpleasant for you. America has taken jazz musicians for granted. Jazz is a dirty word in this country. Europe is saving jazz and it certainly saved my life." [14]

Griffin at least returned home fairly well known through recordings and frequent U.S. appearances. Don Byas was not so lucky. Coming back for the 1970 Newport Jazz Festival, he found two decades of fans who didn't know who he was. When asked a year earlier when he was coming back, Byas replied, "When they build a bridge." [15]

Despite the return of many musicians, the exodus continues (if not with the force it once did) as musicians follow in the footsteps of Sidney Bechet, the first jazz exile to find acceptance and acclaim in the capitals of Europe.

It's not surprising that it took a French director to make 'Round Midnight. The first jazz book was written by a Belgian, Robert Goffin; the second by a Frenchman, Hugues Panassie, and the first in-depth discography by another Frenchman, Charles Delaunay.[16] A park was

Philly Joe Jones (Ken Whitten Collection)

dedicated to drummer Max Roach, but it was not where one might expect, in New York, but in Brixton, England.[17] Charlie Parker Plaza or Duke Ellington Boulevard are yet to materialize in the United States.

Jazz does seem, as Dizzy Gillespie wrote, "too good for America." The numbers alone indicate that Gillespie was correct in saying that "foreign countries have beaten us to the punch in exploiting a music so fully that we originally created." Consequently, the American jazz musician found the cultural climate in Europe was and is far more conducive to artistic expression. Culturally, however, the European view has made the embracing of jazz and its artists no more unusual than the Continent's attitude toward classical composers or painters. The arts are an accepted and enjoyed part of European life, and one has only to stroll around the streets of Paris or Florence to realize the depth of the European artistic tradition.

"Jazz mirrors the very soul of America and has no rival in global reach. The music transcends cultural distinctions and ignores geography," said Andrew Whist of Philip Morris. Musicians have always known this. But racism too has played a role in the defection of American musicians. America's heritage of slavery is absent in Europe, and as singer Jon Hendricks points out, "Europeans don't see black artists as sons of slaves, even subconsciously. That history is simply not there. In Europe, there's a direct line between the artist and the audience that we don't have in America."[18]

Black musicians also did not have to contend with a segregated musicians' union in Europe, nor endure the indignity of performing for white audiences while at the same time being denied hotel rooms. The numbers of black jazz exiles certainly bears this point out, and Johnny Griffin's claim—"Europe is saving jazz and it certainly saved my life"—is heard often.

White jazz musicians were affected by racism quite another way. "The white jazz musician is not really accepted in the center of American society because he or she is regarded as playing black music and black music is not accepted," says Art Farmer.[19] Other musicians, particularly in the sixties, cite political reasons for the exile life. Bassist Red Mitchell is a good example. A resident of Stockholm since 1968, Mitchell was actively engaged in opposition to the Vietnam War. "My efforts added up to little," Mitchell says. "I was contributing more to the opposition through paying taxes. I didn't want to pay taxes anymore and I didn't want to go to jail either. I also didn't want to continue doing movie and television music which I felt was contributing to the atmosphere of violence. From the beginning, I have to take my share of the blame. I was playing on the 'Peter Gunn' show in the late fifties, which was the first in a long series of shoot-'em-ups that used jazz in the background."[20]

Andrew Gurr wrote: "The exiled artist is like the rag which is tied in the middle of the rope used in a tug of war. He marks the still point between two straining forces. From one direction he is pulled by the sense of his own individuality which helped to make him an artist, the distinctive voice ready to tell its audience what they are not yet conscious of. From the other direction comes the tug of the unknown, the blank fear of the exile who has lost that sense of identity which comes from the feeling of belonging in a community."[21]

Finally then, racism, politics, and differing cultural views all contributed to the drain of American talent and set many musicians on a course for foreign shores. Jazz continues to be accepted worldwide. Tokyo, once the adopted home for saxophonist Charlie Mariano, clarinetist Tony Scott, and drummer Donald Bailey, is now a regular stop on the international jazz circuit. Sidney, Stockholm, and Nice continue to be major venues for jazz, and Europe the place many American jazz musicians still call home.

Where then is jazz headed? Art Farmer says, "A person who asks that kind of question usually doesn't have the slightest idea where jazz is."[22]

Jazz still remains largely in Europe, but as Johnny Griffin points out, "America is the source of jazz, and its audiences, when receptive, experience the music at its deepest levels."

When that happens in America, perhaps all the jazz exiles will come home.

Appendix: The Jazz Exiles

The following sample listing of the jazz exiles gives the year of their first tour abroad or the year foreign residence began, their best-known musical associations or the leader on the initial tour, and the country of primary residence while abroad.

Year	Jazz Exile	Associates	Residence
1919	Sidney Bechet	Will Marion Cook	France
1919	Arthur Briggs	Will Marion Cook	France
1919	Louis Mitchell	Will Marion Cook	France/England
1919	Benny Peyton	Will Marion Cook	France
1923	Alberta Hunter	Noble Sissie	France/England
1925	Garvin Bushell	Sam Wooding	France/Germany
1925	Tommy Ladnier	Sam Wooding	France/Germany
1925	Claude Hopkins	Josephine Baker	France
1927	Doc Cheatham	Sam Wooding	France
1927	Dave Tough	Woody Herman	France
1933	Coleman Hawkins	Fletcher Henderson	France
1933	Louis Armstrong	King Oliver	France
1934	Benny Carter	Fletcher Henderson	France/England
1934	Bill Coleman	Duke Ellington	France
1945	Rex Stewart	Duke Ellington	France
1946	Don Byas	Count Basie	Holland
1947	Jay Cameron	Slide Hampton	France/Belgium
1948	Peanuts Holland	Don Redman	France
1948	Gigi Gryce	Clifford Brown	France
1948	Mezz Mezzrow	Sidney Bechet	France
1948	Joe Turner	Adelaide Hall	France
1949	James Moody	Dizzy Gillespie	France
1949	Benny Waters	Jimmy Lunceford	France
1949	Tadd Dameron	Dizzy Gillespie	France
1949	Benny Bailey	Lionel Hampton	Sweden/Germany

Year	Jazz Exile	Associates	Residence
1950	Zutty Singleton	Sidney Bechet	France
1950	Roy Eldridge	Gene Krupa	France
1951	Nat Peck	Clarke-Boland	England
1951	Jimmy Gourley	Jay Burkhart	France
1952	Bob Dorough	Sugar Ray Robinson	France
1953	J. C. Heard	Cab Calloway	Japan
1953	Albert Nicholas	Luis Russell	France
1954	Kansas Fields	Babs Gonzales	France
1955	Jimmy Pratt	Chet Baker	Germany
1955	Chet Baker	Gerry Mulligan	France/Italy
1955	Allan Eager	Tadd Dameron	France
1956	Kenny Clarke	Dizzy Gillespie	France
1956	Quincy Jones	Dizzy Gillespie	France
1958	Oscar Pettiford	Dizzy Gillespie	Sweden
1958	Eddie Sauter	Bill Finegan	Germany
1958	Stan Getz	Woody Herman	Sweden
1958	Bud Powell	Charlie Parker	France
1959	Jimmy Woode	Duke Ellington	Austria
1959	Lucky Thompson	Dexter Gordon	Sweden
1959	Tony Scott	Billie Holiday	Japan/Italy
1961	Kenny Drew	Lester Young	France/Denmark
1961	Idres Sulliman	Quincy Jones	Sweden
1962	Dexter Gordon	Wardell Gray	France/Denmark
1962	Mark Murphy	Michel Legrand	England/Holland
1962	Donald Byrd	Pepper Adams	France
1962	Nathan Davis	Kenny Clarke	France
1962	Sonny Criss	Gerald Wilson	France
1963	Johnny Griffin	Thelonious Monk	Holland
1963	Leo Wright	Dizzy Gillespie	Germany
1963	Sahib Shihab	Quincy Jones	Sweden
1963	Carmel Jones	Gerald Wilson	Germany
1963	Art Taylor	John Coltrane	France
1963	Herb Geller	Chet Baker	Germany
1965	Albert Heath	J.J. Johnson	Denmark

Year	Jazz Exile	Associates	Residence
1965	Stuff Smith	Dizzy Gillespie	Denmark
1965	Lee Konitz	Lennie Tristano	Denmark
1965	Mal Waldron	Billie Holiday	Germany
1965	Hal Singer	Lucky Milinder	France
1965	Don Cherry	Ornette Coleman	France
1966	Jiggs Wigham	Stan Kenton	Germany
1967	Randy Weston	Kenny Dorham	Morocco
1967	Steve Lacy	Thelonious Monk	France/Italy
1967	Jimmy Heath	Art Farmer	Sweden
1968	Philly Joe Jones	Miles Davis	England/France
1968	Phil Woods	Quincy Jones	France
1968	Slide Hampton	Maynard Ferguson	Sweden
1968	Richard Boone	Count Basie	Sweden/Denmark
1968	Art Farmer	Benny Golson	Austria
1968	Dave Pike	Herbie Mann	Germany
1968	Jon Hendricks	L, H & R	England
1968	Maynard Ferguson*	Stan Kenton	England
1968	Sy Oliver	Jimmy Lunceford	France
1968	Clifford Jordan	Horace Silver	Germany
1968	Hank Mobley	Miles Davis	France
1968	Burton Greene	Don Cherry	Belgium/Holland
1968	Red Mitchell	Hampton Hawes	Sweden
1968	Tony Inzalaco	Maynard Ferguson	Germany
1969	Ted Curson	Cecil Taylor	Sweden
1969	Anthony Braxton	Ornette Coleman	France
1969	Roscoe Mitchell	Art Ensemble	France
1970	Lou Blackburn	Gerald Wilson	Germany
1971	Charlie Mariano	Toshiko Akiyoshi	Holland
1972	Ed Thigpen	Oscar Peterson	Denmark
1973	Horace Parlan	Charles Mingus	Denmark
1974	Bud Freeman	Yank Lawson	England

*Although Canadian, Ferguson has been so much a part of the American jazz scene that he is included here.

Year	Jazz Exile	Associates	Residence
1975	John Duke	Count Basie	Sweden
1977	Walter Norris	Thad Jones-Lewis	Germany
1978	Donald Bailey	Hampton Hawes	Japan
1979	Thad Jones	Mel Lewis	Sweden
1979	John Clayton	Count Basie	Holland
1980	Dee Dee Bridgewater	Jones/Lewis	France
1980	Ernie Wilkins	Count Basie	Denmark
1983	Don Rader	Maynard Ferguson	Germany
1988	Bill Takas	Bob Dorough	France
1989	Sal Nistico	Woody Herman	Germany

Notes

Preface

1. Andrew Gurr, *Writers in Exile: The Identity of Home in Modern Literature* (Brighton, Sussex, England: Harvester Press, 1983), pp. 17–19.
2. James Lincoln Collier, *Duke Ellington* (New York: Oxford University Press, 1987), p. 152.
3. Ibid., p. 193.
4. Ibid., p. 155.
5. James Lincoln Collier, *The Reception of Jazz in America: A New View*, monograph no. 27 (New York: Institute for Studies in American Music, 1988), p. 27.
6. Ibid.

Prelude

1. Frederick S. Starr, *Red and Hot: The Fate of Jazz in the Soviet Union* (New York: Oxford University Press, 1983), pp. 37–38.
2. Leonard Feather, "A Master at Work," *Jazz Times*, Oct. 1988, p. 38.
3. Zane Knauss, *Conversations with Jazz Musicians* (Detroit: Gale Research Co., 1977), p. 233.

Chapter I: The Road to Europe

1. Bechet's reluctance to join Cook on this European tour was well known and produced a number of versions of how the clarinetist was enticed to accompany the Southern Syncopated Orchestra to England.
2. Michael Zwerin, "Jazz Triste," *Esquire's World of Jazz* (New York: Thomas Crowell Co., 1975), pp. 188–194.
3. Jon Hendricks, Personal Interview, 1981.
4. Dizzy Gillespie "Jazz Is Too Good For America," *Esquire's World of Jazz*, pp. 168–175.
5. Lee Jeske, "Jazz in Europe," *Downbeat*, Feb. 9, 1978.
6. Mark Murphy, Personal Interview, 1981.
7. Bud Freeman, Personal Interview, 1981.

8. Eddie "Lockjaw" Davis, Personal Interview, 1980.

9. Kitty Grime, ed., *Jazz at Ronnie Scott's* (London: Robert Hale, 1979).

10. Phil Woods, Personal Interview, 1981.

Chapter 2: Early Explorers

1. Chris Goddard, *Jazz Away from Home* (London: Paddington Press, 1979), p. 22.

2. James Lincoln Collier, *The Making of Jazz: A Comprehensive History* (Boston: Houghton Mifflin, 1978), p. 128.

3. Goddard, *Jazz Away from Home*, p. 52. Goddard is quoting from *Jazz Hot*, May 1969, in which Jean Christophe Averti wrote that Bechet was jumped on the steps of the Shelburne Hotel in Chicago.

4. John Chilton, *Sidney Bechet: The Wizard of Jazz* (New York: Oxford University Press, 1989).

5. Ernest Ansermet in *Frontiers of Jazz*, ed. Ralph de Toledano (New York: Frederick Unger, 1946), pp. 121–122.

6. Gunther Schuller, *Early Jazz* (New York: Oxford University Press, 1968), pp. 194–198.

7. Goddard, *Jazz Away from Home*, pp. 30–52.

8. The information on Bechet's life is taken from several sources: Collier, Goddard, Simon, and Bechet's own biography, *Treat It Gentle*.

9. Goddard, *Jazz Away from Home*, pp. 30–52.

10. John Chilton, *Sidney Bechet*, p. 97.

11. Ibid., p. 246.

12. Ibid., pp. 232–233.

13. Ibid., p. 277.

14. Goddard, *Jazz Away from Home*, p. 78.

15. Ibid., p. 78.

16. George Simon, *The Best of the Music Makers* (New York: Doubleday, 1979), p. 134.

17. William H. Kenney 3d, "The Assimilation of Jazz in France, 1917–1940," *American Studies*, vol. 15 no. 1, Spring 1984, p. 6.

18. George Simon, *The Best of the Music Makers*, p. 134.

19. Lee Jeske, "Alberta Hunter—Singer of Songs," *Downbeat*, January 1980.

20. Frank C. Taylor with Gerald Cook, *Alberta Hunter: A Celebration in Blues* (New York: McGraw Hill Books, 1987), pp. 260–261, 275, 278.

21. According to Bud Freeman, Dave Tough and F. Scott Fitzgerald often wrote limericks together at Bricktop's.

22. Goddard, *Jazz Away from Home*, pp. 30–52.

23. The British Musicians' Union prevented Carter from playing in England, a problem drummer Philly Joe Jones also experienced in 1968.

24. Edward Berger, *Benny Carter: A Life in American Music* (New Jersey: Scarecrow Press, 1982), p. 145.

25. James Collier, *The Making of Jazz: A Comprehensive History* (Boston: Houghton Mifflin, 1978), pp. 146–147.

Chapter 3: Garvin Bushell

1. Official birth records show Bushell's birth date to be 1902.

2. Bushell also toured Europe in 1959 with Wilbur De Paris and Africa in 1964 with Paul Taubman.

3. Bassist Montgomery operated the Las Vegas Jazz Society until 1983. He also conducted interviews with Bushell for the Smithsonian.

Chapter 4: Bud Freeman

1. Chris Goddard, *Jazz Away from Home* (London: Paddington Press, 1979), p. 67.

2. *New Yorker* profile.

3. The writer for both the Freeman and Clarke interviews was Helen Oakley Dance.

Chapter 5: The Modern Exiles

1. Michael Zwerin, "Jazz Triste," *Esquire's World of Jazz* (New York: Thomas Crowell, 1975), p. 87.

2. Zwerin, "Jazz Triste," pp. 188–194.

3. Lee Jeske, "James Moody's Move," *Downbeat*, July 1980.

4. Ira Gitler, *Jazz Masters of the Forties* (New York: Macmillan, 1966), pp. 22–24.

5. "Jazz Musicians in Europe," *Time*, May 1963.

6. Ira Gitler, "Chet Baker's Tale of Woe," *Downbeat*, July 30, 1960.

7. "Back from the Dark Side," *Time*, April 17, 1964.

8. Ira Gitler, "Chet Baker: A Farewell," *Jazz Times*, July 1988.

9. Edwart Hotaling, "French Want Only Own Jazz," *The New York Times*, Dec. 19, 1965.

10. Leonard Feather, "Expatriates Riffin' Back Home," *Los Angeles Times*, Oct. 29, 1978.

11. Hollie I. West, "The Jazz Man's Bittersweet Return," *The Washington Post,* Sept. 29, 1979, pp. 100–101.
12. Gary Giddins, "Johnny Griffin: An American in New York," *Village Voice,* Oct. 23, 1978, pp. 9–10.
13. Zan Stewart, "Griffin," *Musician/Player & Listener,* Feb. 1979.

Chapter 8: Art Farmer

1. Whitney Balliet, *The New Yorker,* Sept. 23, 1985, pp. 43–55.

Chapter 10: Eddie "Lockjaw" Davis

1. Las Vegas, where Davis made his home, is a case in point. KNPR-FM, the public radio affiliate, opted to discontinue its jazz programing and go to an all-classical format in 1989. The jazz record collection, however, was turned over to the University of Nevada, Las Vegas, station, KUNV-FM.

Chapter 11: Phil Woods

1. Kirk Silsbee, *The Jazz Review,* February 1992, pp. 56–58.
2. Zane Knauss, *Conversations with Jazz Musicians* (Detroit: Gale Research, Inc., 1977), p. 233.
3. Woods discusses his experiences in Japan in a later chapter.

Chapter 12: Jon Hendricks

1. "Ofays" was an often-heard pig latin term for Caucasian.
2. Hendricks made a number of appearances on British DJ Simon Dee's show, which had as its studio band an orchestra led by trumpeter Maynard Ferguson.
3. Annie Ross appeared in two major films, *Superman* and *Yanks.*
4. According to Hendricks, the album wound up costing $120,000.

Chapter 13: Nathan Davis

1. Davis is referring to the film *Lady Sings the Blues* with Diana Ross.

Chapter 15: Donald "Duck" Bailey

1. Bailey is referring to the difference between the four-to-the-bar beat of jazz as opposed to the heavy back-beat on two and four of rock music.
2. The "they" Bailey refers to in much of this conversation is the powers of the music business.

Coda

1. Robert Wolf, "Bud Freeman," *Downbeat*, Sept. 1986, p. 49.
2. Ira Gitler, " 'Round Midnight," *Jazz Times*, Oct. 1986, pp. 14–16.
3. Samuel G. Freedman, "The Blues of Expatriate Paris: Recalling America's Jazz Exiles," *The New York Times*, Oct. 12, 1986, pp. 1, 16.
4. "Horns of Plenty," *Time*, Oct. 22, 1990, p. 66.
5. Ibid.
6. Ibid.
7. Ross Russell, *Bird Lives: The High Life and Hard Times of Charlie "Yardbird" Parker* (New York: Charterhouse Press, 1973), p. 272.
8. Lynn Darroch, "Nothing Limits Me Now," *Jazz Times*, Apr. 1985, pp. 12–13.
9. Zane Knauss, *Conversations with Jazz Musicians* (Detroit: Gale Research Inc., 1977), p. 257.
10. Mike Hennessey, "Europajazz," *Jazz Times*, June 1986, p. 8.
11. Whitney Balliet, "Art Farmer," *The New Yorker*, Sept. 23, 1985, pp. 43–55.
12. Whitney Balliet, "Walter Norris," *The New Yorker*, Jan. 12, 1987, pp. 88–91.
13. Francis Davis, "An American in Paris," *Atlantic Monthly*, Nov. 1989, pp. 120–124.
14. Dempsey Travis, *An Autobiography of Black Jazz* (Chicago: Urban Research Institute, Inc., 1983), pp. 361–362.
15. Arthur Taylor, *Notes and Tones* (New York: Perigee Books, 1977), pp. 44–45.
16. "Soundings," *Jazz Times*, July 1986, p. 3.
17. Grover Sales, *Jazz: America's Classical Music* (New Jersey: Prentice Hall, 1986), p. 83.
18. Jon Hendricks interview.
19. Farmer's statement is from the video *Jazz in Exile*. On-camera interviews with Phil Woods, Slide Hampton, Dexter Gordon, Johnny Griffin, and Woody Shaw are in the film as well.
20. Red Mitchell, "News," *Downbeat*, June 7, 1979, p. 9.
21. Andrew Gurr, *Writers in Exile: The Identity of Home in Modern Literature* (New Jersey: Humanities Press, 1983), p. 33.
22. Nat Hentoff, liner notes for The Jazztet, *Real Time*, Contemporary Records, 1986.

Bibliography

Ansermet, Ernest. *Frontiers of Jazz*. Ed. Ralph de Toledano. New York: Frederick Unger, 1946.

Bailey, Donald. Phone Interview, 1992.

Balliett, Whitney. "Art Farmer." *The New Yorker*, 23 September 1985, pp. 43–55.

Bechet, Sidney. *Treat It Gentle*. London: 1960.

Berger, Morroe, Edward Berger, and James Patrick. *Benny Carter: A Life in American Music*. Metuchen, N.J.: Scarecrow Press and the Institute of Jazz Studies, Rutgers University, 1982.

Bushell, Garvin, as told to Mark Tucker. *Jazz from the Beginning*. Ann Arbor: University of Michigan Press, 1988.

Cameron, Jay. Personal Interview, 1990.

Chilton, John. *Sidney Bechet: The Wizard of Jazz*. New York: Oxford University Press, 1987.

———. *Who's Who of Jazz: Storyville to Swing Street*. London: Chilton Books, 1970.

Coleman, Bill. *Trumpet Story*. Boston: Northeastern University Press, 1990.

Collier, James Lincoln. *The Making of Jazz: A Comprehensive History*. Boston: Houghton Mifflin, 1978.

———. "The Faking of Jazz." *New Republic*, 18 November 1985, pp. 33–39.

Cowley, Malcolm. *Exile's Return: A Literary Odyssey of the 1920s*. New York: Penguin Books, 1986.

Darroch, Lynn. "Nothing Limits Me Now." *Jazz Times*, April 1985.

Davis, Eddie. Personal Interview, August 1980 and April 1986.

Davis, Francis. "An American in Paris." *Atlantic Monthly*, November 1989.

Davis, Nathan. Telephone Interview, May 1991.

Davis, Ursula Broschke. *Paris Without Regret*. University of Iowa Press, 1986.

Dempsey, Travis. *An Autobiography of Black Jazz*. Chicago: Urban Research Institute, Inc., 1983.

Dorough, Bob. Telephone Interview, June 1990.

Farmer, Art. Telephone Interview, May 1990.

Feather, Leonard. *The Encyclopedia of Jazz in the Sixties*. New York: Horizon Press, 1966.

France, Chuck. *Jazz in Exile*. New York: Rhapsody Films, 1986.

Freedman, Samuel G. "The Blues of Expatriate Paris: Recalling America's Jazz Exiles." *The New York Times*, 12 October 1986.

Freeman, Lawrence. Personal Interview, November 1980 and October 1986.

Gillespie, Dizzy. "Jazz Is Too Good for America." *Esquire's World of Jazz*. New York: Thomas Crowell, 1960.

Gitler, Ira. " 'Round Midnight." *Jazz Times*, October 1986, pp. 14–16.

———. *Jazz Masters of the Forties*. New York: Macmillan, 1966.

Goddard, Chris. *Jazz Away from Home*. London: Paddington Press, 1979.

Hennessey, Mike. "Europa Jazz." *Jazz Times*, June 1986, p. 8.

"Jazz Musicians in Europe." *Time*, 17 May 1963.

Jeske, Lee. "James Moody's Move." *Downbeat*, July 1980.

———. "Alberta Hunter—Singer of Songs." *Downbeat*, January 1980.

Knauss, Zane. *Conversations with Jazz Musicians*. Detroit: Gale Research Co., 1977.

Leonard, Neil. *Jazz: Myth and Religion*. New York: Oxford University Press, 1987.

Mezzrow, Milton, with Bernard Wolfe. *Really the Blues*. New York: Dell Publishing, 1946.

Mitchell, Red. Telephone Interview, October 1991.

Morgenstern, Dan. *Jazz People*. New York: Harry N. Abrams, 1976.

Murphy, Mark. Personal Interview, November 1980.

Russell, Ross. *Bird Lives! The High Life and Hard Times of Charlie "Yardbird" Parker*. New York: Charterhouse Press, 1973.

Sancton, Thomas. "Horns of Plenty." *Time*, 22 October 1990.

Sales, Grover. *Jazz: America's Classical Music*. New Jersey: Prentice Hall, 1986.

Schuller, Gunther. *Early Jazz*. New York: Oxford University Press, 1968.

Simon, George T. *The Best of the Music Makers*. New York: Doubleday, 1979.

Starr, S. Frederick. *Red and Hot: The Fate of Jazz in the Soviet Union*. New York: Oxford University Press, 1983.

Taylor, Arthur. *Notes and Tones*. New York: Perigee Books, 1977.

Taylor, Frank C., with Gerald Cook. *Alberta Hunter: A Celebration in Blues*. New York: McGraw Hill Books, 1987.

Tiegel, Eliot. "Trinkle Tinkle Little Star." *Pulse*, October 1990.

Wolf, Robert. "Blindfold Test—Bud Freeman." *Downbeat*, September 1986.

Woods, Phil. Personal Interviews, November 1980 and March 1981.

Zwerin, Michael. "Jazz Triste," in *Esquire's World of Jazz*. New York: Thomas Crowell Co., 1975.

Index